About this book

KU-178-376

This Practice Workbook contains questions to target every topic in P2/3 English.

Questions split into three levels of increasing difficulty – Challenge 1, Challenge 2 and Challenge 3 – to aid progress.

Symbols to highlight questions that test grammar, punctuation and spelling skills.

Total marks boxes for each challenge and topic.

'How am I doing?' checks for self-evaluation.

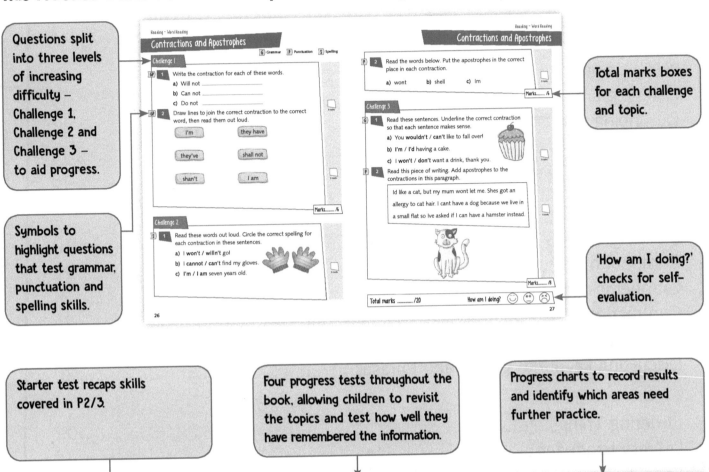

Starter test recaps skills covered in P2/3.

Four progress tests throughout the book, allowing children to revisit the topics and test how well they have remembered the information.

Progress charts to record results and identify which areas need further practice.

Answers for all the questions are included in a pull-out answer section at the back of the book.

Author: Lynn Huggins-Cooper

Contents

Contents

ACKNOWLEDGEMENTS

The author and publisher are grateful to the copyright holders for permission to use quoted materials and images.

Every effort has been made to trace copyright holders and obtain their permission for the use of copyright material. The author and publisher will gladly receive information enabling them to rectify any error or omission in subsequent editions. All facts are correct at time of going to press.

Published by Leckie
An imprint of HarperCollins*Publishers*
Westerhill Road
Glasgow G64 2QT
HarperCollins*Publishers*
1st Floor, Watermarque Building, Ringsend Road
Dublin 4, Ireland

© 2017 Leckie

ISBN 9780008250218

First published 2017

10 9 8 7 6 5 4

All rights reserved. No part of this publication may be reproduced, stored in a retrieval system, or transmitted, in any form or by any means, electronic, mechanical, photocopying, recording or otherwise, without the prior permission of Collins.

British Library Cataloguing in Publication Data.

A CIP record of this book is available from the British Library.

Series Concept and Development: Michelle I'Anson
Commissioning and Series Editor: Chantal Addy
Author: Lynn Huggins-Cooper
Project Manager and Editorial: Rebecca Rothwell
Cover Design: Sarah Duxbury
Inside Concept Design: Ian Wrigley
Text Design and Layout: Contentra Technologies
Artwork: Collins and Contentra Technologies
Production: Natalia Rebow
Printed by CPI Group (UK) Ltd, Croydon CR0 4YY

Starter Test

S **1.** Fill in the missing letters to complete the names of the days of the week.

a) Mo <u>n d a</u> y

b) T <u>u e</u> <u>s d</u> ay

c) <u>W</u> ednes <u>d d</u> y

d) Th <u>u r s</u> d <u>a</u> y

e) F <u>r</u> i <u>d</u> a <u>y</u>

f) <u>S</u> at <u>u r</u> d <u>a</u> y

g) Su <u>n d</u> ay

7 marks

2. Fill in the missing letters in each set.

a)

j	k	l	<u>m</u>	<u>n</u>	o	p	q

b)

c	d	e	<u>f</u>	<u>g</u>	<u>h</u>	i	j	k

c)

i	j					o	p	q

d)

r	s	t				x	y	z

e)

t	u	v				z

5 marks

4

6 **3.** Add the prefix **un–** to these words.

Example: happy ⟶ unhappy

a) done ⟶ _____

b) cooked ⟶ _____

c) fair ⟶ _____

d) tied ⟶ _____

4 marks

4. Copy these capital letters neatly in your best handwriting.

a) ABCD _____

b) EFGH _____

c) IJKL _____

d) MNOP _____

e) QRST _____

f) UVW _____

g) XYZ _____

7 marks

P **5.** Rewrite the sentences adding capital letters and full stops.

a) the lady sat on the chair

_____

b) the horse jumped over the fence

_____

c) the hedgehog slept in the leaves

_____

d) the bath filled with bubbles

_____

4 marks

6. These words need capital letters. Write the capital letters above the letters that need changing to correct the words.

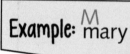

Example: M̌mary

a) london   **b)** tuesday   **c)** sue

d) rajan   **e)** rome   **f)** saturday

6 marks

P **7.** Add the missing exclamation marks.

a) It's cold__

b) That's nasty__

c) How rude__

d) How awful—

e) That's so smelly—

5 marks

P **8.** Add the missing question marks.

a) What's the time—

b) Can I come—

c) What's your name—

d) Do you like ice cream—

e) What's that sound—

5 marks

9. Break these words into their syllables.

Example: hedgehog ⟶ h e d g e / h o g

a) rabbit ⟶ _ _ _ / _ _ _ _ _

b) tortoise ⟶ _ _ _ _ / _ _ _ _ _ _

c) kangaroo ⟶ _ _ _ _ / _ _ _ / _ _ _ _

d) | lion | ⟶ _ _ / _ _

e) | tiger | ⟶ _ _ / _ _ _

5 marks

10. Circle the word in each pair which has a **–tch** sound.

a) | page | | pitch |

b) | patch | | panda |

c) | home | | hutch |

d) | fade | | fetch |

e) | kitchen | | kennel |

5 marks

G ⟩ **11.** Add the suffix **–er** to these words.

a) | catch | ⟶ _____

b) | pitch | ⟶ _____

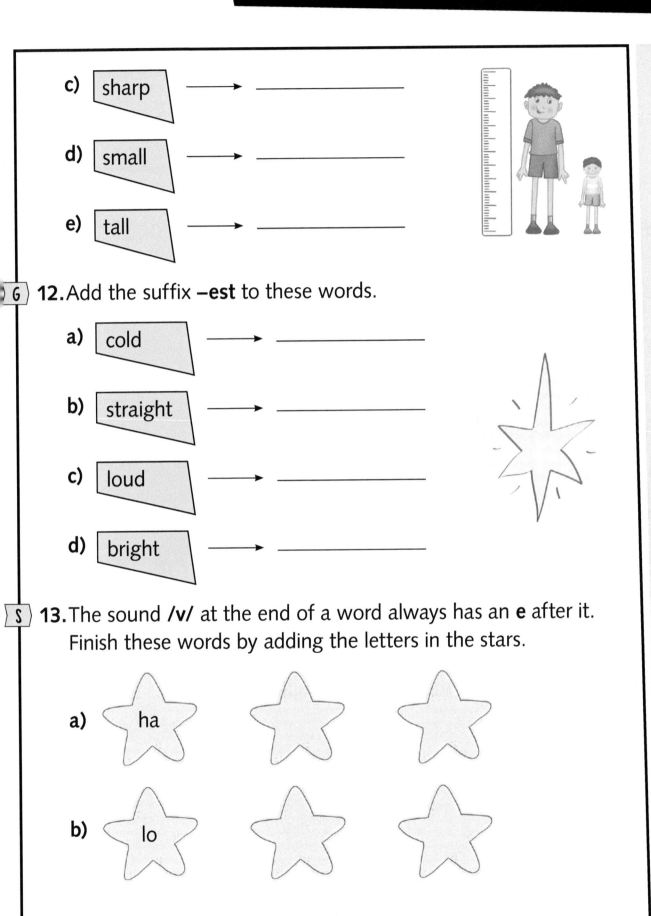

c) sharp ⟶ _____

d) small ⟶ _____

e) tall ⟶ _____

5 marks

G **12.** Add the suffix **–est** to these words.

a) cold ⟶ _____

b) straight ⟶ _____

c) loud ⟶ _____

d) bright ⟶ _____

4 marks

S **13.** The sound **/v/** at the end of a word always has an **e** after it. Finish these words by adding the letters in the stars.

a) ha

b) lo

c)

li

d)

glo

e)

gi

5 marks

S **14.** Fill in the **ff** to complete the words.

a) flu __ __

b) sta __ __

c) stu __ __

d) cu __ __

e) blu __ __

5 marks

S **15.** Fill in the missing **ss** on the circles to complete the words.

a) fu

b) me

c) pre

d) cre

e) stre

5 marks

S **16.** Fill in the missing **zz** to complete the words.

a) fu __ __

b) bu __ __

c) mu __ __le

d) nu __ __le

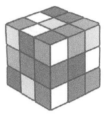

e) pu __ __le

5 marks

S **17.** Join the two words together to make a new word.

a) butter + flies = _____

b) rattle + snake = _____

c) him + self = _____

d) grass + hopper = _____

e) basket + ball = _____

f) fire + works = _____

g) air + port = _____

h) skate + board = _____

8 marks

Marks........ /90

11

Listening and Asking Questions

Challenge 1

1 Talk to a friend about their favourite TV show.
Listen carefully to what they say. Can you remember what they said afterwards?

5 marks

2 Talk to a grown up about what games they played when they were a child. Ask questions and listen carefully to what they have to say.

5 marks

Marks......... /10

Challenge 2

1 Ask a friend to tell you how to make something – a model or something similar. Ask questions to make sure you understand what they say. Then try to write down the instructions on a separate piece of paper. Can you follow the instructions?

5 marks

Listening and Asking Questions

2 Ask a grown-up to tell you how to carry out a job in the house, like using the washing machine. Ask questions if you need to. Can you remember what to do afterwards?

5 marks

Marks......... /10

Challenge 3

1 Visit your favourite museum with a grown-up. Look at an exhibit that really interests you – it could be about animals, Egyptians, science – whatever you like best! Ask one of the museum guides at least five questions about the exhibit to find out more.

5 marks

2 At the library, think of a particular subject you want to find out about, and ask a librarian to help you. You could ask questions about the books and where they are stored, as well as finding out how to search on the computer for the sort of books you need.

5 marks

Marks......... /10

Total marks .... /30   How am I doing?

Describing and Explaining

Challenge 1

1 Describe your favourite TV programme to your parents. Tell them about the characters or presenters, the setting and the ideas. Explain what you like about the programme and why it is your favourite.

5 marks

2 Explain to a friend how to play your favourite game. Describe it in as much detail as you can. What equipment do you need to play it? Where can you play it? How many people can play it at once? How long can it be played for? Explain why it is your favourite.

5 marks

Marks......... /10

Challenge 2

1 Describe your ideal birthday.
- What would you do?
- Where would you go?
- If you had a party, explain what it would be like.
- What would your birthday cake look like?
- What would your ideal gifts be?

5 marks

Describing and Explaining

2 Explain to your friend how to look after a pet.
What do they eat? How do they get exercise? What toys do they play with? How do you keep them healthy? What equipment do they need?

5 marks

Marks......... /10

Challenge 3

1 Play a drawing game with a friend. Take turns to describe a made-up animal and the other person has to draw it. Think of five things each to say about the way your animal looks.

5 marks

2 Explain how to make an ice lolly from fresh juice and fruit.
- What things do you need?
- How would you prepare the fruit?
- How would you add the juice?
- How long would it take the lolly to freeze?
- How would you get the lolly out of the mould?

5 marks

Marks......... /10

Total marks .... /30   How am I doing?

Telling Stories and Narrating

Challenge 1

1 Tell someone about your journey to school in at least five different steps. Tell them what happens between leaving your house and arriving at school – in the right order!

5 marks

2 Tell someone about the best holiday you have ever had. Tell them about where you went, where you stayed and your favourite activities. Don't forget the food you liked to eat, and to talk about the journey home!

5 marks

Marks......... /10

Challenge 2

1 Retell a famous fairy tale out loud. Can you remember all of the characters, what they do and the things that happen during the story? Make sure the story is told in the correct order!

5 marks

Telling Stories and Narrating

2 Tell a joke. Do you have a favourite? If not, ask your friends what jokes they like best and see if you can learn them – and then tell the joke to someone else! See if you can make them laugh! Remember – jokes need to be told in the correct order so they make sense.

5 marks

Marks......... /10

Challenge 3

1 Tell a parent or grown-up about your day at school, from start to finish. Tell them about:
- The work you did in the morning.
- What you played at playtime.
- What you ate for lunch.
- What activities you did in the afternoon.
- What happened at home time.

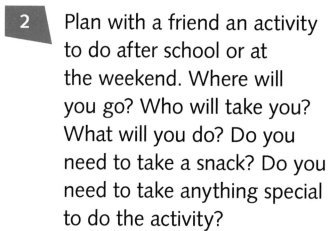

5 marks

2 Plan with a friend an activity to do after school or at the weekend. Where will you go? Who will take you? What will you do? Do you need to take a snack? Do you need to take anything special to do the activity?

5 marks

Marks......... /10

Total marks .... /30

How am I doing?

Role-play and Opinions

Challenge 1

1 Imagine you are a zookeeper taking children around the zoo on a tour.
Tell them all about the different opinions on zoos – 'pros' (the good things) and 'cons' (the bad things). Do zoos help with the conservation of animals (keep them safe and breed more)? Is it cruel to keep animals in captivity instead of out in the wild?

5 marks

2 Today, you are interviewing a sports star. Ask a friend to role play as the star. Think of five questions you would like to ask.

5 marks

Marks......... /10

Challenge 2

1 Imagine that you are a teacher encouraging the children in your class to play outdoors more. Give reasons why it is important to spend time outdoors. What fun things can you do outside that you can't do inside?

5 marks

Role-play and Opinions

2 Make up a presentation about your favourite animal. Collect pictures and find out facts about your chosen animal. You could use toys or models to help with your presentation. Become an expert and tell your family and friends all of the things you have found out!

Begin your presentation by telling your audience what you are going to talk about. Then tell them why this animal is your favourite. Offer lots of facts about your animal and let your audience ask questions at the end.

5 marks

Marks......... /10

Challenge 3

1 With a friend or grown up, imagine you are at the beach when you find a strange creature sitting in a rock pool. It asks for your help. You are shocked and amazed – so what do you do next? What do you say? Try to imagine all of the questions you could ask the creature about its life and where it has come from.

5 marks

2 Some people say that children watch too much television. How do you feel about that? Imagine that you have to give a speech in assembly about this.

- Do you think TV is a bad thing?
- Do you think some programmes are a good thing?
- Can you learn things from TV?
- Is television just something that fills your time?

Make up your own mind, once you have thought about these questions. Can you see both sides of the argument?

5 marks

Marks......... /10

Total marks .... /30   How am I doing?

19

Blending Sounds

Challenge 1

1 Lots of words begin with the letter blend **bl**. Circle the words that begin with **bl** in each set.

a) blue, green, black, grey

b) blade, brood, blood, board

c) blend, boat, bleat, bread

3 marks

2 Words can begin and end with the blend **st** – and have them in the middle too! Underline the words in each group that use the blend **st**.

a) stamp, drink, stink, dark

b) must, fast, master, mist

c) last, make, take, test

3 marks

Marks.......... /6

Challenge 2

1 Lots of words begin with the letter blend **dr**. Tick the words in each set that begin with **dr**.

a) drip ☐   door ☐   drink ☐   dark ☐

b) drill ☐   daft ☐   drum ☐   damp ☐

c) dress ☐   duck ☐   date ☐   drop ☐

3 marks

Blending Sounds

2 The letter blend **ph** makes the sound **f**. Underline the words that use the letter blend **ph**.

a) graph, fall, elephant, laugh

b) phrase, staff, gnat, photo

c) phone, phantom, fellow, giraffe

3 marks

Marks.......... /6

Challenge 3

1 The blend **th** can be found in lots of words in the beginning, in the middle and at the end. Circle the words that use the blend **th**.

a) those, shop, bath, shoes

b) that, these, shape, trap

c) path, sink, then, trust

3 marks

2 Tick the words that use the blend **gr**.

a) growl ☐   gate ☐   grape ☐

b) grind ☐   giggle ☐   glad ☐

c) grate ☐   gnat ☐   grab ☐

3 marks

Marks.......... /6

Total marks .... /18   How am I doing?

Compound Words

G Grammar   P Punctuation   S Spelling

Challenge 1

S | 1 Add the two words to make a compound word.

a) straw + berry = _____

b) post + card = _____

c) light + house = _____

3 marks

S | 2 Match the words in each list by joining them with a line.
Write the compound words.

a) table   ache   _____

b) cross   roads   _____

c) tooth   cloth   _____

3 marks

Marks.......... /6

Challenge 2

S | 1 Look at the pictures. What compound words do they make?

a)  + ⚽ = _____

b) 🦶 + 🏞️ = _____

c) 💪 + 🪑 = _____

3 marks

GS | 2 Make three compound words of your own.

a) _____

b) _____

c) _____

3 marks

Marks.......... /6

Compound Words

Challenge 3

GS 1 Work out the meaning of these compound words by splitting them into their parts.

> **Example:** birdhouse = **bird** + **house** so a birdhouse is a house for birds.

a) paintbrush = _____ + _____

so 'paintbrush' means _____.

b) rainbow = _____ + _____

so 'rainbow' means _____.

c) handmade = _____ + _____

so 'handmade' means _____.

3 marks

GS 2 Try to work out the meaning of these words from the meaning of the root words. You can check the meanings in a dictionary.

> **Example: Arbor** means tree, so **arboreal** means 'to do with trees,' or 'lives in trees.'

a) **Sol** means sun. **Solar** means _____

b) **Therm** means heat. **Thermometer** means

_____

c) **Vac** means empty. **Vacuum** means _____

3 marks

Marks.......... /6

Total marks .... /18   How am I doing?

23

Graphemes and Phonemes

Challenge 1

1 Circle the grapheme **ai** in these words. Read the words out loud.

a) chain, care, paint

b) stain, mare, faint

c) pain, rain, dare

3 marks

2 Circle the grapheme **ee** in these words. Read the words out loud.

a) feet, beat, fate

b) great, seen, rate

c) deep, shape, shop

3 marks

Marks.......... /6

Challenge 2

1 Write a sentence that contains each of these **ie** words.

a) believe _____

_____

b) field _____

_____

c) shriek _____

_____

3 marks

Graphemes and Phonemes

2 Tick the grapheme **ei**. Say these words. What do they mean?

a) deceive ☐ leave ☐ career ☐

b) feeding ☐ receipt ☐ mountain ☐

c) brave ☐ creek ☐ receive ☐

3 marks

Marks.......... /6

Challenge 3

1 Write a sentence containing each word in the box to show that you know what they mean.

survey	maybe	stain

a) _____

_____

b) _____

_____

c) _____

_____

3 marks

2 Write sentences with words that use these graphemes.

a) **ie** _____

_____

b) **ee** _____

_____

c) **ea** _____

_____

3 marks

Marks.......... /6

Total marks .... /18   How am I doing?

Contractions and Apostrophes

G Grammar **P** Punctuation **S** Spelling

Challenge 1

GP **1** Write the contraction for each of these words.

a) Will not _____

b) Can not _____

c) Do not _____

3 marks

GP **2** Draw lines to join the correct contraction to the correct word, then read them out loud.

I'm   they have

they've   shall not

shan't   I am

3 marks

Marks.......... /6

Challenge 2

S **1** Read these words out loud. Circle the correct spelling for each contraction in these sentences.

a) I **won't / willn't** go!

b) I **cannot / can't** find my gloves.

c) **I'm / I am** seven years old.

3 marks

Contractions and Apostrophes

P **2** Read the words below. Put the apostrophes in the correct place in each contraction.

a) wont **b)** shell **c)** Im

3 marks

Marks.......... /6

Challenge 3

G **1** Read these sentences. Underline the correct contraction so that each sentence makes sense.

a) You **wouldn't / can't** like to fall over!

b) **I'm / I'd** having a cake.

c) I **won't / don't** want a drink, thank you.

3 marks

P **2** Read this piece of writing. Add apostrophes to the contractions in this paragraph.

Id like a cat, but my mum wont let me. Shes got an allergy to cat hair. I cant have a dog because we live in a small flat so Ive asked if I can have a hamster instead.

5 marks

Marks.......... /8

Total marks .... /20   How am I doing?

Prefixes and Suffixes

G Grammar   P Punctuation   S Spelling

Challenge 1

GS **1** Draw a line to join the root word to the suffix.

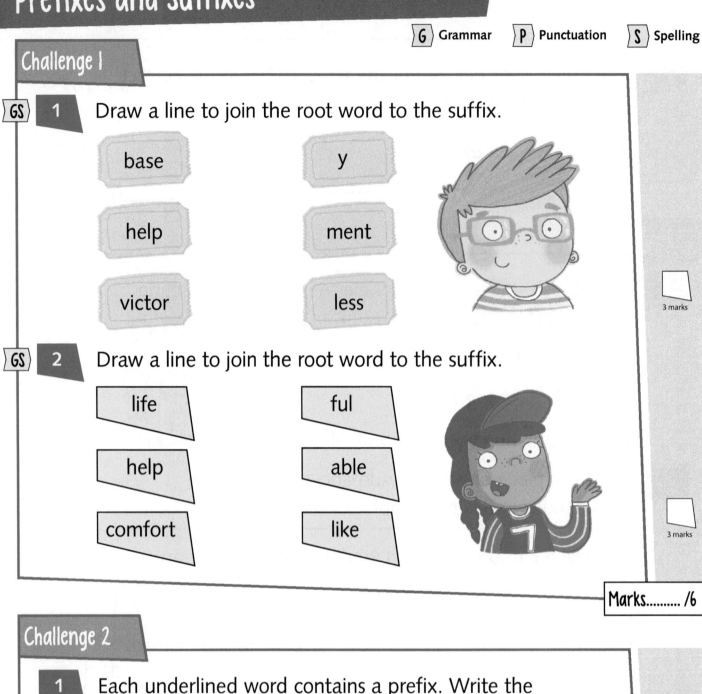

base	y
help	ment
victor	less

3 marks

GS **2** Draw a line to join the root word to the suffix.

life	ful
help	able
comfort	like

3 marks

Marks.......... /6

Challenge 2

1 Each underlined word contains a prefix. Write the meaning of each underlined word below.

a) The <u>unmade</u> bed looked messy.

_____

b) I can <u>retake</u> my test if I need to.

_____

c) That was rather <u>impolite</u>!

_____

3 marks

Prefixes and Suffixes

2 Now try these words.

a) I really <u>dislike</u> that sour taste!

_____

b) That is <u>unbelievable</u>!

_____

c) This film is a <u>remake</u> of an old film.

_____

3 marks

Marks.......... /6

Challenge 3

G **1** Write a suffix on the end of each of these words to make a new word. It could be **–ment**, **–ness** or **–ful**.

a) amaze_____

b) dry_____

c) sad_____

3 marks

G **2** Write a root word to complete these suffixes.

a) _____ment

b) _____ful

c) _____ness

3 marks

Marks.......... /6

Total marks .... /18   How am I doing?

Discussing Favourite Words and Phrases

Challenge 1

1 Look at these words. Circle your favourite word in each list.

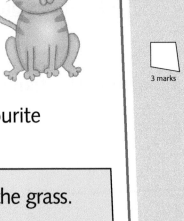

a) leathery, scaly, furry, spiny

b) bubbly, fizzy, foamy, fluffy

c) giggle, howl, laugh, squeak

3 marks

2 Now read this passage. Choose your three favourite phrases and underline them.

> The fox peeped out of the leaves. It could see food on the grass.
>
> The fox started to drool, and his eyes sparkled. There were juicy
>
> apples, sweet cakes and best of all a chicken leg. They were just
>
> sitting there on a piece of red material. Humans were odd creatures.

3 marks

Marks.......... /6

Challenge 2

1 Read these sentences. Circle your favourite word in each one, and explain why in the space below.

a) The dragon roared and spit fire into the darkness of the cave.

_____

b) The spider slid down a thread of silk, and dangled in the breeze.

_____

Discussing Favourite Words and Phrases

c) The juice poured down my chin, as I crunched the shiny green apple.

_____

3 marks

2 Now read this paragraph. Choose and underline your two favourite phrases, then write about why you chose them in the space below.

> The boy looked into the velvet-dark sky. Stars glittered there, and the boy thought about other worlds, out there in space. He wondered if there were mountains and grainy deserts. He stroked the silky cat that curled around his legs, and wondered if there were strange, purple space cats with wings.

_____

_____

_____

_____

3 marks

Marks.......... /6

Challenge 3

1 Make a 'Favourite Words and Phrases' jotter. Take a plain notebook and decorate it however you want. You could paste pieces of newspaper and magazine on the cover so there are lots of words! As you read, and come across words and phrases you like the sound of, note them down in your jotter. This will make you a better reader – and writer!

6 marks

Marks.......... /6

Total marks .... /18   How am I doing? 😊 😐 😣

Ordering Things

1 These pictures tell the story of *Three Billy Goats Gruff* but they are in the wrong order! Number them correctly from 1–5.

5 marks

Marks.......... /5

Ordering Things

1 Use the pictures to retell the story of *Goldilocks and the Three Bears*.

Write the story on a separate sheet of paper.

1

2

3

4

5

6

6 marks

Marks.......... /6

1 Imagine you are the wicked queen from *Snow White and the Seven Dwarfs* and you have been arrested for your crimes! Retell the story from your point of view.

Write your story on a separate sheet of paper.

5 marks

Marks.......... /5

Total marks .... /16   How am I doing?

Literary Language

1 Fiction is a story that has been made up by the author. Picture books and chapter books are both types of fiction.

a) What is your favourite fiction book?

_____

b) How do you know it is fiction?

_____

c) How is fiction different to non-fiction?

_____

3 marks

Marks........../3

1 Non-fiction books often contain fact boxes pictures and special features to tell you about a subject.

a) Do you enjoy reading non-fiction books? Explain your answer.

_____

b) Look at a non-fiction book from the school library (or one of your own). What special features can you see on the pages?

_____

c) What is your favourite non-fiction book? Explain your answer.

_____

3 marks

Marks........../3

Literary Language

1 Science fiction is about new technology – sometimes in space, sometimes in the future. It doesn't have to be about space, aliens and spaceships though! An example is *The Iron Man* by Ted Hughes.

a) What makes a book science fiction?

_____

b) Are all science fiction books about space?

_____

c) Name the title and author of a science fiction book for young readers.

_____

3 marks

2 Books in the humour genre are funny. They have silly ideas, jokes and funny action that makes the reader laugh. An example is the *Diary of a Wimpy Kid* series by Jeff Kinney.

a) Choose a humorous story you have read. Why was it funny?

_____

b) How did you know it was a funny story? Explain your answer.

_____

c) Name two humorous books or series.

_____

3 marks

Marks.......... /6

Total marks .... /12   How am I doing?

Reading Non-fiction

Challenge 1

1 Read this non-fiction paragraph about the beach and answer the questions.

> When the tide is out, many things are left on the strand line. You might see live creatures, such as crabs and tiny insects as well as winkles and other shellfish. You can also see crab shells, empty shells, cuttlefish bones and feathers. Sadly, you can also find litter such as fishing line and plastic bottles.

a) What live creatures might you find on a strand line?

_____   _____

_____   _____

b) Name three other natural things you might find on the strand line.

_____   _____

_____   _____

c) What sort of litter can be found on the strand line?

_____   _____

3 marks

Marks........../3

Challenge 2

1 Read the paragraph and answer the questions.

> Rainbows happen when it rains and is sunny at the same time. The colours of the rainbow are red, orange, yellow, green, blue indigo and violet. You can remember the colours of the rainbow with the mnemonic Richard Of York Gave Battle In Vain.

Reading Non-fiction

a) Name four colours that can be found in the rainbow.

_____   _____

_____   _____

b) When do we see rainbows?

_____

c) What mnemonic can be used to remind yourself of the colours of the rainbow? Can you learn it?

_____

3 marks

Marks............/3

Challenge 3

1 Read this passage and answer the questions

> Nocturnal animals are active at night. Bats are nocturnal. They fly at night, hunting for food. Hedgehogs and badgers are also nocturnal, as are owls. People can go on specially organised night walks with wildlife wardens and animal charities to spot these animals.

a) What are nocturnal animals?

_____

b) Name three nocturnal animals. _____

_____   _____

c) Who might organise special night-time activity walks for people to see nocturnal animals?

_____   _____

3 marks

Marks............/3

Total marks ..../9   How am I doing?

Reading Fiction

Challenge 1

1 Read this paragraph and answer the questions below.

Lucas imagined that he was a spaceman. He put a bowl on his head as his helmet, and shone his torch at the ceiling to make stars. When the dog walked into the room, he imagined it was an alien!

a) What did Lucas imagine he had become?

_____

b) What did he use as a helmet?

_____

c) Who did Lucas imagine the dog had become?

_____

3 marks

Marks........../3

Challenge 2

1 Read the paragraph and put the missing words in the sentences that follow.

Livvy was playing in the garden. She saw a mouse pop through a hole in the wall. Then she saw it come back, carrying a shiny red berry in its mouth. She watched as the mouse made a pile. Finally, it sat down next to the berries and started to eat.

Reading Fiction

a) Livvy was playing in the _____.

b) She saw a _____ pop through a hole in the wall.

c) The mouse was carrying a _____.

3 marks

Marks............/3

Challenge 3

1 Read this paragraph and answer the questions below.

> Lulu wanted to be a pirate. She longed to sail on the Seven Seas and fight sea serpents. She wanted to find buried treasure. She dreamed of wearing big golden earrings and a stripy red jersey. For now though, that would have to wait. It was time for school.

a) What does Lulu want to be?

_____

b) What did Lulu want to wear?

_____

c) What did Lulu want to do on the Seven Seas?

_____

3 marks

Marks............/3

Total marks ..../9

How am I doing?

Finding Meaning

Challenge 1

1 Read this passage and answer the questions.

> The boy trudged down the street, dragging his feet. He couldn't be bothered to go. It had been fine yesterday, before they'd laughed at him. Now he would rather stay at home.

a) How is the boy feeling?

_____

b) What words describing his movements give you a clue to his feelings?

_____

c) Why do you think the boy would rather stay at home?

_____

3 marks

Marks............/3

Challenge 2

1 Read this piece of writing and answer the questions below.

> The sky was its usual grey but it was colder. Huge white flakes, like feathers, began to fall. The girl held her hand up in amazement. She had never seen anything like it before. What were these lumps of cold fluff falling from the sky?

a) What are the white things falling from the sky?

_____

b) Why do you think the girl is so surprised at the weather?

_____

Finding Meaning

c) What time of year do you think it is?

_____

3 marks

Marks............/3

Challenge 3

1 Read this paragraph and answer the questions.

> I couldn't eat my tea. I felt a bit sick and excited at the same time. I couldn't wait. I couldn't believe we were going after all this time. I had begun to believe that we just wouldn't go, despite all of my dreaming and begging. I wanted to go on the rides, and to see the characters walking around. I couldn't wait!

a) Where do you think the child wants to go?

_____

b) How do you know that they have wanted to go for a long time?

_____

c) How is the child feeling? Explain in your own words.

_____

3 marks

Marks............/3

Total marks ..../9

How am I doing?

Learning About Poetry

Challenge 1

1 Narrative poems tell a story. They often rhyme which makes them easier to understand.

The Rime of the Ancient Mariner is a good example of a narrative poem. Read this out loud and answer the questions.

> Day after day, day after day,
> We stuck, nor breath nor motion;
> As idle as a painted ship
> Upon a painted ocean.

a) What does a narrative poem do?

_____

b) What makes narrative poems easier to remember?

_____

c) Write the two words that rhyme in the poem.

_____

3 marks

Marks............/3

Challenge 2

1 Shape or concrete poetry is written in the shape of the subject of the poem. A poem about snakes could be written in a wiggly line, and a poem about leaves could be written in a leaf shape.

The scaly snake slithered through the soaking grass.

a) What is another name for a shape poem?

_____

Learning About Poetry

b) What is a shape poem? _____

_____

c) What shape could a poem about trees be written in?

_____

3 marks

Marks.......... /3

 Nonsense poetry uses made-up words to create a poem.

Make up some words to fit these subjects.

a) Swamp – make the words sound squelchy and smelly, like 'stenchilicious'!

b) Alligator – make the words sound toothy or scaly, like 'daggerysharp'!

c) Frog – make the words sound springy and croaky, like 'sproingy'!

d) Now write a nonsense poem using your own made-up words! Write your poem on a separate piece of paper.

4 marks

Marks.......... /4

Total marks .... /10

How am I doing?

Getting Information from Instructions and Lists

Challenge 1

1 Read the instructions and answer the questions.

> To make a tasty cheese sandwich, take two slices of bread and spread them thinly with pickle. Carefully cut slices of cheese with a knife and place them between the slices of bread. Cut the sandwich in half and serve it with some salad.

 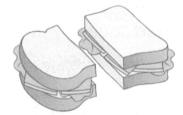

a) What can you spread on the bread?

_____

b) What do you serve with the sandwich?

_____

c) What does the passage suggest you cut cheese with?

_____

3 marks

Marks............/3

Challenge 2

1 Read this list and write the missing 'gem' words in the crystals.

Diamond, ruby, emerald, opal, topaz, aquamarine and garnet.

Getting Information from Instructions and Lists

a) The third gem is

b) The fifth gem is

c) The last gem is

3 marks

Marks............/3

Challenge 3

 Read these instructions for making an owl stick puppet, then answer the questions.

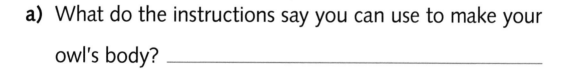

Draw a rounded shape on scrap card to make your owl's body. You can use old packaging. Cut two leaf shapes for wings. Paint or colour the owl, and stick the wings on the sides of the puppet. Add big circles cut from card or paper to make eyes, and a triangle to make a beak. Tape a lolly stick to the back of your puppet – and play!

a) What do the instructions say you can use to make your owl's body? _____

b) What can you make the eyes from? _____

c) What shape is the beak? _____

3 marks

Marks............/3

Total marks ..../9

How am I doing?

Getting Information from Dialogue

Challenge 1

1 Read this conversation and answer the questions.

> 'What's that?' asked Samira.
>
> 'It's a dibber,' said Grandma. 'I use it to poke holes in the soil to plant my seeds.'
>
> 'What sort of seeds are you planting?' Samira asked, looking at the packets.
>
> 'Carrot, broccoli and cauliflower,' said Grandma. 'To make lovely dinners with.'

a) Who was planting seeds? _____

b) What tool was Grandma using to plant seeds?

_____

c) Name the seeds that Grandma was planting.

_____

3 marks

Marks............/3

Challenge 2

1 Plays don't use speech marks. Read this conversation from a play and answer the questions. Use full sentences for your answers.

> **Alex:** Let's take the puppies out for a walk!
> **Leigh:** Great! Shall we take them down by the river?
> **Alex:** Oh yes – they love seeing the ducks and geese – they get really excited.
> **Leigh:** Do you remember when Daisy rolled in that mud and she looked like a brown dog?
> **Alex:** I do – it was so funny. Then Ellie jumped in the leaves and found a frog.
> **Leigh:** I think she thought it was a toy!

Getting Information from Dialogue

a) Where are Alex and Leigh going for a walk?

_____

b) Name the two types of bird that the puppies like to see.

_____

c) What did Daisy roll in? _____

3 marks

Marks............/3

Challenge 3

1 Read the conversation and answer the questions.

> 'I'd like six apples and a bunch of bananas please.'
> 'Would you like a bag?'
> 'No thanks – I have a cloth bag here. They can go in there.'
> 'Anything else today?'
> 'I'd like this punnet of strawberries and four large oranges please.'
> 'That will be £5.56 please.'
> 'There you go – thanks!'

a) How many oranges does the customer want to buy?

_____

b) What is the customer's bag made from? _____

c) How many apples does the customer buy? _____

3 marks

Marks............/3

Total marks ..../9   How am I doing?

Progress Test 1

1. Talk to a friend about their favourite film. Ask two questions and listen to their answers. Write down their answers.

   1. _____

   2. _____

   2 marks

2. Explain why you like your favourite toy or game. What makes it so interesting?

   _____

   _____

   2 marks

3. Describe your last holiday or day out. What did you enjoy? Was there anything you did not enjoy?

   _____

   _____

   2 marks

4. Do you think children spend enough time playing outside? Do you think they spend too much time indoors, watching TV and playing on the computer? Explain your views.

   _____

   _____

   2 marks

P **5.** Add the possessive apostrophes to the underlined words.

a) The <u>d o g s</u> ears are floppy.

b) The <u>b o y s</u> teddy was brown.

c) The <u>w o m a n s</u> hair was blonde.

3 marks

6. Pretend you are a reporter reporting for the news about the story of *Rumpelstiltskin*. Retell this traditional tale.

_____

_____

_____

_____

_____

_____

_____

_____

4 marks

7. Read this passage and answer the questions.

> Wasps make their nests out of chewed-up wood. They chew fences, garden furniture and sheds, and mix this wood with saliva to make a papery nest. The queen builds the nest, starting with one cell, in the spring. It is often built in the roof space of a house, or from a beam in a shed or garage.

a) What are wasp nests made from?

_____

b) What is the wood mixed with?

_____

c) Who starts the nest in the spring?

_____

d) Name two places a wasp nest might be built.

_____

4 marks

8. Read these instructions and answer the questions.

> To make easy peppermint creams, you need icing sugar, water, a drop of green food colouring and some peppermint essence. Mix the ingredients together in a bowl. Sprinkle a little icing sugar on a kitchen surface and form the dough into a lump. Roll the dough flat, and cut shapes with small cutters. Decorate them with green sprinkles. Leave the sweets to set and dry a little before eating.

a) What ingredients do you need to make peppermint creams?

_____

b) What do you add to the icing sugar to flavour it?

_____

c) When you have mixed the ingredients into a dough, what is the next step?

_____

d) What can the sweets be decorated with?

_____

4 marks

Marks........./23

Breaking Words into Segments

Challenge 1

S **1** Look at these **ss** words. Show how you would break these words into chunks to learn the spellings.

> **Example:** grass ⟶ gr + ass

a) fuss ⟶ _____ + _____

b) class ⟶ _____ + _____

c) stress ⟶ _____ + _____

3 marks

S **2** Look at these **ch** words. Show how you would break these words into chunks to learn the spellings.

> **Example:** pitch ⟶ p + i + tch

a) perch ⟶ _____ + _____ + _____

b) church ⟶ _____ + _____ + _____

c) much ⟶ _____ + _____

3 marks

Marks.......... /6

Challenge 2

S **1** Try these **sp** words. Show how you would break these words into chunks to learn the spellings.

> **Example:** spin ⟶ sp + in

a) crisp ⟶ _____ + _____

b) wasp ⟶ _____ + _____

c) spider ⟶ _____ + _____

3 marks

Breaking Words into Segments

S **2** Try these **st** words. Show how you would break these words into chunks to learn the spellings.

| **Example:** | stick ⟶ st + ick |

a) stand ⟶ _____ + _____

b) fast ⟶ _____ + _____

c) waste ⟶ _____ + _____

3 marks

Marks.......... /6

Challenge 3

S **1** Try these **th** words. Show how you would break these words into chunks to learn the spellings.

| **Example:** | thick ⟶ th + ick |

a) thump ⟶ _____ + _____

b) moth ⟶ _____ + _____

c) fifth ⟶ _____ + _____

3 marks

S **2** Try these **zz** words. Show how you would break these words into chunks to learn the spellings.

| **Example:** | jazz ⟶ j + azz |

a) whizz ⟶ _____ + _____

b) fizz ⟶ _____ + _____

c) buzz ⟶ _____ + _____

3 marks

Marks.......... /6

Total marks .... /18

How am I doing?

Syllables

G Grammar   **P** Punctuation   **S** Spelling

Challenge 1

1 These are words with two syllables. Read them out loud. Can you hear the two syllables? Write the syllables down on the lines.

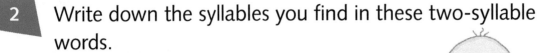

a) table   _ _ / _ _ _

b) paper   _ _ / _ _ _

c) smiling _ _ _ / _ _ _ _

3 marks

2 Write down the syllables you find in these two-syllable words.

a) baby   _ _ / _ _

b) donkey _ _ _ / _ _ _ _

c) rabbit   _ _ / _ _ _ _

3 marks

Marks.......... /6

Challenge 2

1 These are words with three syllables. Read them out loud. Can you see what the three syllables are? Write the syllables down on the lines.

a) animal   _ _ / _ / _ _ _

b) dinosaur _ _ / _ _ / _ _ _ _

c) pelican   _ _ _ / _ / _ _ _

3 marks

54

2 Write down the syllables you find in these three-syllable words.

a) September _ _ _ / _ _ _ _ / _ _ _

b) October _ _ _ / _ / _ _ _

c) November _ _ / _ _ _ _ / _ _ _

3 marks

Marks......... /6

Challenge 3

1 Circle the words that have three syllables.

| telephone | Friday | Saturday |
| radio | Tuesday | Monday |

3 marks

2 Write the number of syllables next to each word.

a) ladybird _____

b) spider _____

c) slug _____

3 marks

Marks......... /6

Total marks .... /18

How am I doing?

Homophones

G Grammar   P Punctuation   S Spelling

Challenge 1

G **1** Choose the correct homophone. Circle the word that makes sense.

a) It was a dark and stormy **night / knight**.

b) At **night / knight**, bats fly around my garden.

c) The **night / knight** swung his sword.

d) A suit of armour is worm by a **night / knight**.

4 marks

G **2** Which **bee / be** is the right **bee / be**? Circle the word you choose.

a) A **bee / be** landed on my nose!

b) When will you **bee / be** ready?

c) When will it **bee / be** my turn?

d) **Bee / Be** careful!

4 marks

Marks.......... /8

Challenge 2

G **1** Choose the right word so the sentence makes sense. Circle the correct word.

a) **They're / There / Their** not coming with us.

b) That's **they're / there / their** fault!

c) What's that over **they're / there / their**?

d) Our dogs loved **they're / there / their** walk today.

4 marks

Challenge 2

G | **2** Underline the correct **see / sea** in each sentence.

a) I can hear the **see / sea**!

b) I can **see / sea** you.

c) I like playing in the sand,
by the **see / sea**.

d) **See / Sea** if you can find the treasure.

4 marks

Marks.......... /8

Challenge 3

G | **1** Choose the correct word. Underline the word you choose.

a) My favourite fairy **tale / tail** is Cinderella.

b) The dragon's **tale / tail** had a pointy end.

c) Rosie, my dog, loves to chase her **tale / tail**.

d) Grandpa loves to tell me a **tale / tail** before bed.

G | **2** Choose the right word – **accept** or **except**?
Circle your choice.

a) I like everything **except / accept** cabbage.

b) I can't **except / accept** that token for that ride.

c) We are all coming **except / accept** Jay.

d) I will **except / accept** my trophy.

4 marks

4 marks

Marks.......... /8

Total marks .... /24   How am I doing?

Spelling – The Beginnings of Words

G Grammar **P** Punctuation **S** Spelling

Challenge 1

S **1** Say these words out loud. Underline the words which have a silent **g** or **k** at the beginning of the words.

a) not, gnat, nice

b) gnome, no, not

c) nag, knit, none

d) need, needle, knot

4 marks

S **2** The following words are missing the **wr**. Fill in the missing letters.

a) That is the _____ong answer.

b) I _____ote my name on my notebook.

c) I saw a worm _____iggle.

3 marks

Marks.......... /7

Challenge 2

GS **1** Write a word with a silent letter at the beginning from the box into each of these sentences, so they make sense.

| gnat | knot | knitted | knight |

a) I _ _ _ _ _ _ _ a hat.

b) She swatted the _ _ _ _ with a newspaper.

c) The _ _ _ _ _ _ put on his armour.

d) I tied a _ _ _ _.

4 marks

Spelling – The Beginnings of Words

S **2** Copy these words and learn to spell them. Use LOOK, COVER, WRITE, CHECK to help you.

a) wrestle _____

b) wrist _____

c) wrinkle _____

3 marks

Marks.......... /7

Challenge 3

S **1** Circle the words in this paragraph that have a silent **g** or **k** at the beginning of them.

The gnat and the dragonfly flew over the pond. A knot of grass hung over the edge of the water, next to a gnome. The gnat flew close to a butterfly and knocked into her wing. "Sorry!" he called.

5 marks

S **2** Colour in the wrapped parcels that contain **wr** words.

wring

ring

ran

wrong

rang

wing

2 marks

Marks.......... /7

Total marks .... /21   How am I doing?

Spelling – The Ends of Words

G Grammar   P Punctuation   S Spelling

Challenge 1

S **1** Underline the correct spelling.

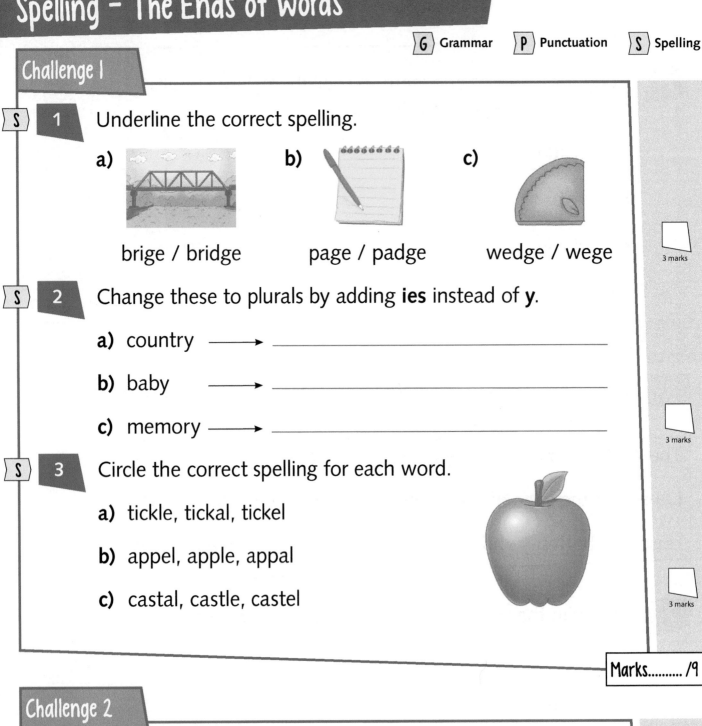

a)

brige / bridge

b)

page / padge

c)

wedge / wege

3 marks

S **2** Change these to plurals by adding **ies** instead of **y**.

a) country ⟶ _____

b) baby ⟶ _____

c) memory ⟶ _____

3 marks

S **3** Circle the correct spelling for each word.

a) tickle, tickal, tickel

b) appel, apple, appal

c) castal, castle, castel

3 marks

Marks.......... /9

Challenge 2

S **1** Copy these words and learn to spell them. Use LOOK, COVER, WRITE, CHECK to help you.

a) edge _____

b) judge _____

c) lodge _____

3 marks

Spelling – The Ends of Words

S **2** Change these words from plural to singular.

a) valleys _____

b) surveys _____

c) monkeys _____

3 marks

S **3** Join the correct ending to the beginning of each word with a line.

eag   al

trav   el

dent   le

3 marks

Marks.......... /9

Challenge 3

S **1** Underline the correct spelling in each sentence.

a) I like orange **lollys / lollies** best.

b) I went to the beach on my **holidays / holidaies**.

c) I lost my **keys / keies**.

3 marks

S **2** Write the correct ending of these words in these sentences.

a) I ate my dinner at the tab_____.

b) Use a tow_____to dry your hands.

c) Add the numbers to find the tot_____.

3 marks

Marks.......... /6

Total marks .... /24   How am I doing? ☺ 😐 😣

Spelling – Exception Words

G) Grammar   P) Punctuation   S) Spelling

Challenge 1

S **1** Learn to spell these common exception words that all use the same pattern. Remember LOOK, COVER, WRITE, CHECK. Then write a sentence containing each word.

a) cold _____

b) gold _____

c) fold _____

3 marks

S **2** Now learn these exception words. Write a sentence for each word to show that you know what they mean.

a) last _____

b) past _____

c) father _____

3 marks

Marks.......... /6

Challenge 2

S **1** Which words in each set are exception words (words that don't follow the rules)? Circle them.

a) patting, fixing, slapping

b) mixing, matting, mapping

c) sitting, boxing, clapping

3 marks

2 Write a sentence that contains each set of three exception words.

a) pretty, everybody, grass

_____

_____

Spelling – Exception Words

b) class, plant, water

_____

_____

c) break, move, parents

_____

_____

3 marks

Marks.......... /6

Challenge 3

S **1** We can use mnemonics (things to help jog your memory using the first letter of each word in a sentence) to remind us how to spell unusual exception words.

Write the words being spelled out here.

a) **B**ig **E**lephants **C**an **A**lways **U**nderstand **S**mall **E**lephants

_____

b) **S**ome **U**mbrellas **G**et **A**ll **R**ipped _____

c) **C**an **L**ittle **O**wls **T**ell **H**ow **E**ggs **S**it _____

3 marks

S **2** Make up a mnemonic for these exception words – then learn them!

a) every _____

b) whole _____

c) beautiful _____

3 marks

Marks.......... /6

Total marks .... /18

How am I doing?

Handwriting – Spacings and Sizes

Challenge 1

1 Copy the letters on the lines.

a) abc _____

b) def _____

c) ghi _____

3 marks

2 Write a line of the lower case version of the letter next to the capital given.

a) M _____

b) G _____

c) R _____

3 marks

3 Now write a line of the capital letter next to the lower case letter given.

a) d _____

b) x _____

c) y _____

3 marks

Marks.......... /9

Challenge 2

1 Copy these words. Be careful about spacing the letters.

a) and _____

b) can _____

c) cup _____

3 marks

2 Copy the names below on to the lines. Be careful to make the letters the right size, with capital letters bigger than lower case letters.

a) Andrew _____

Handwriting – Spacings and Sizes

b) Rajan _____

c) Sophia _____

3 marks

Marks.......... /6

Challenge 3

1 Copy these words. Be careful about spacing the letters.

a) name _____

b) time _____

c) page _____

d) mime _____

e) came _____

f) door _____

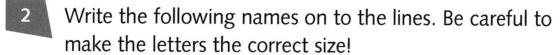

6 marks

2 Write the following names on to the lines. Be careful to make the letters the correct size!

a) Your full name

_____

b) Your best friend's name

_____

c) The name of your favourite pop star

_____

3 marks

Marks.......... /9

Total marks .... /24

How am I doing?

65

Handwriting – Joins

Challenge 1

1 Copy these words using joined-up handwriting. Do not join letters that are not joined in the word.

a) *progress* _____

b) *super* _____

c) *horse* _____

3 marks

2 Copy these horizontal joins using joined-up handwriting. Repeat to fill the line.

a) *oi* _____

b) *oy* _____

c) *oa* _____

3 marks

Marks.......... /6

Challenge 2

1 Copy these words using joined-up handwriting. Do not join letters that are not joined in the word.

a) *question* _____

b) *baby* _____

c) *project* _____

3 marks

2 Copy these diagonal joins using joined-up handwriting. Repeat to fill the line.

a) *ir* _____

b) *ur* _____

c) *er* _____

3 marks

Marks.......... /6

Handwriting – Joins

Challenge 3

1 Copy these words using joined-up handwriting. Do not join letters that are not joined in the word.

a) soft   _____

b) hope   _____

c) craft   _____

d) loft   _____

e) people   _____

f) packing   _____

6 marks

2 Copy these diagonal joins using joined-up handwriting. Repeat to fill the line.

a) ea   _____

b) dis   _____

c) ice   _____

d) ode   _____

e) ole   _____

f) ere   _____

6 marks

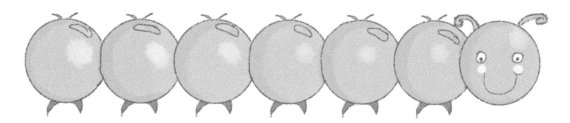

Marks.........../12

Total marks ..../24   How am I doing?

S **1.** Look at these **ch** words. Show how you would break these words into chunks to learn the spellings.

     a) chase   ⟶   _____ + _____

     b) chicken ⟶   _____ + _____

     c) chirp   ⟶   _____ + _____

     d) pinch   ⟶   _____ + _____

4 marks

2. Underline your favourite word in each sentence. Explain why you chose each word.

     a) I saw a huge, spiky spider crab.

     _____

     b) The rain is drumming on the car roof.

     _____

     c) The crunchy lettuce in this sandwich is delicious!

     _____

d) When Dad vacuumed, there were enormous dust bunnies made of dog hair!

_____

4 marks

6 **3.** Choose the right homophone for each sentence. Draw a circle round the correct word.

a) I want to come **to / two / too**.

b) I saw a **bare / bear** at the zoo.

c) **Their / There / They're** was a mouse in the kitchen!

d) Look over **their / there / they're**!

e) **Their / There / They're** best friends with my brother.

5 marks

P **4.** Add the possessive apostrophes to the underlined words.

a) The l i o n s teeth were enormous.

b) The g i r l s trainers are very muddy.

c) The c h i l d r e n s books are stacked neatly.

4 marks

69

 **G** Grammar   **P** Punctuation   **S** Spelling

G **5.** Choose a **–dge** word from the box to complete each sentence.

sludge	fudge	sledge	dodged	stodgy

a) My favourite sweetie is _____.

b) There was _____ in the bottom of the bath.

c) I _____ the ball as it shot towards me!

d) I like using my _____ in the snow.

e) The food was really _____.

5 marks

S **6.** Change the singular to plural.

a) baby ⟶ _____

b) candy ⟶ _____

c) fairy ⟶ _____

d) diary ⟶ _____

4 marks

7. Practise your handwriting. Copy and repeat these letters using joined-up handwriting.

a) *or* _____

b) *ot* _____

c) *mag* _____

d) *eer* _____

4 marks

8. Break these words into their syllables.

Example: potato ⟶ p o / t a / t o

a) tomato ⟶ _ _ _ / _ / _ _

b) alligator ⟶ _ _ _ / _ / _ _ / _ _ _

c) terrified ⟶ _ _ _ / _ _ / _ _ _ _

d) waterfall ⟶ _ _ / _ _ _ / _ _ _ _

e) escalator ⟶ _ _ _ / _ / _ _ / _ _ _

5 marks

Writing for Different Purposes – Instructions, Lists and Letters

G Grammar   **P** Punctuation   **S** Spelling

Challenge 1

1 Write the instructions for your favourite playground game here. Make sure they are in the right order.

Name of game: _____

How to play it: 1. _____

2. _____

3. _____

4. _____

5. _____

5 marks

G **2** These sentences use **and** too many times. Write them out again, swapping commas for the extra **ands**.

a) I like apples and oranges and bananas and satsumas.

_____

b) I bought a hat and socks and hankies and gloves.

_____

c) The dog chased pigeons and crows and seagulls and starlings.

_____

_____

3 marks

Marks.......... /8

Challenge 2

P **1** Using the pictures to help you, write a list of what each person bought at the shops. Don't forget your commas!

a)

Writing for Different Purposes – Instructions, Lists and Letters

Jane bought _____

_____

b)

Leon bought _____

_____

2 marks

GPS 2 Write a letter to a new pen pal. Tell them all about your family, and the town where you live. Use a separate piece of paper.

5 marks

Marks.......... /7

Challenge 3

GPS 1 Write instructions for making a model of an animal. You could make it from anything you want – clay, wool or junk. Write down the things you would need, and the steps you would need to take to make the finished model. Use a separate piece of paper.

5 marks

GPS 2 Write a letter to the local newspaper, telling them about an exciting thing you saw happen in your town. Use a separate piece of paper.

5 marks

Marks.......... /10

Total marks .... /25

How am I doing?

Writing About Real Events

G Grammar   P Punctuation   S Spelling

Challenge 1

GPS 1   Write down your memories of your best family outing ever! What happened? Where did you go? Who were you with? What did you do? Did you have special food?

_____

_____

_____

_____

_____

_____

_____

_____

_____

_____

5 marks

Marks.......... /5

Challenge 2

GPS 1   Write a report on a science experiment you carried out at school, or at home. Try to remember the way things happened in order. What results did you collect at the end of the experiment?

_____

_____

Writing About Real Events

_____

_____

_____

_____

5 marks

Marks.......... /5

Challenge 3

GPS | 1 | Write a report on a celebration or festival that you have enjoyed. Write about any parades or parties and report on decorations, special food, clothing or gifts that are given.

_____

_____

_____

_____

_____

5 marks

Marks.......... /5

Total marks .... /15   How am I doing?   😊   😐   😣

Writing Poetry

G) Grammar   P) Punctuation   S) Spelling

Challenge 1

1 Underline all of the words that rhyme in pairs in this poem.

> Humpty Dumpty sat on the wall,
> Humpty Dumpty had a great fall.
> All the king's horses and all the king's men,
> Couldn't put Humpty together again.

4 marks

GPS) **2** Now write a short poem where lines one and two each end in a word that rhymes, and lines three and four each end in a word that rhymes – just like Humpty Dumpty!

_____

_____

_____

_____

4 marks

Marks.......... /8

Challenge 2

1 You are going to write a short poem about monsters. Write down all of the words you can think of to do with monsters on a separate sheet of paper.

3 marks

2 Write the answers to these questions. They will help you to think of ideas to use in your poem.

a) Where does your monster live?

_____

b) Is your monster kind, or mean? How do you know?

_____

Writing Poetry

c) What does your monster eat? Try to think of strange or unusual things, like lost socks or old spider webs.

_____

3 marks

3 Now write your poem on a separate sheet of paper. Use lots of descriptions to make the reader 'see' your monster. Is your poem going to be funny? Is it going to use rhyme? It's up to you – because you are the poet!

10 marks

Marks......... /16

Challenge 3

GS **1** Add your own words to complete this poem about the sunshine.

The sun _____ my face.

It glows in the sky, like a hot yellow _____.

I love the sunbeams that _____ through the trees.

The sun on my skin feels like warm _____.

4 marks

GPS **2** Write a poem about colours. Fill in the spaces with a description of something that is the colour being described. Red could be 'a ladybird shining on a strawberry-velvet rose.'

Yellow is _____.

Blue is _____.

Green is _____.

Brown is _____.

Purple is _____.

5 marks

Marks......... /9

Total marks .... /33   How am I doing?

Planning

Challenge 1

1 Practise your story planning skills by planning a story about a magical world. Use a separate piece of paper. Use the story planning chart below to make short notes about characters, setting and plot.

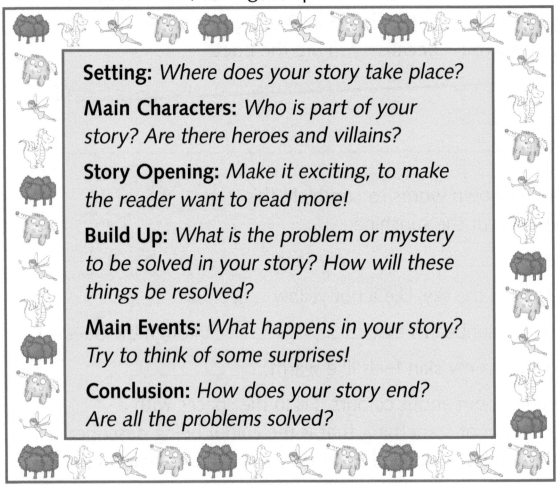

Setting: *Where does your story take place?*

Main Characters: *Who is part of your story? Are there heroes and villains?*

Story Opening: *Make it exciting, to make the reader want to read more!*

Build Up: *What is the problem or mystery to be solved in your story? How will these things be resolved?*

Main Events: *What happens in your story? Try to think of some surprises!*

Conclusion: *How does your story end? Are all the problems solved?*

6 marks

Marks.......... /6

Challenge 2

1 Design and draw your setting on a separate piece of paper. Add in detail a description of where your story is set. What is the landscape like? Are there any buildings? What is the weather like? Think of a place you know well, and describe it using your plan either in words or pictures.

3 marks

Marks.......... /3

Planning

Challenge 3

1 Are there any animals, or people in your magical world? What are they like? Do they look anything like humans or real animals? Are they different colours? Do they have special magical powers? Describe them on a separate piece of paper.

3 marks

2 Make a character planning chart on a separate piece of paper. This should describe your main character in detail. You can also do this as an 'interview', where you ask your character questions and fill in the answers. What sort of questions could you ask?

> Describe your character's physical shape. *Are they tall or short, muscly or slim?*
>
> How do they dress? *What is their hair like?*
>
> Describe their face, and some of the expressions they use. *Do they smile or frown a lot?*
>
> What is your character's voice like? Can you think of a simile to describe it? *Example: 'His voice rumbled in his chest, like a bear growling.'*
>
> How does your character act? *Do they have any special skills or powers?*
>
> Sketch your character.

3 marks

Marks.......... /6

Total marks .... /15   How am I doing?

Similes and Metaphors

Challenge 1

1 Underline the **simile** in each sentence.

a) The caterpillar was as green as a lettuce leaf.

b) The sun was as yellow as a sunflower.

c) The moon looked like a silver coin.

3 marks

2 Write a **simile** about each word.

a) ice _____

_____

b) slug _____

_____

2 marks

Marks.......... /5

Challenge 2

1 Underline the **metaphor** in each sentence.

a) The stars were glitter, thrown across the sky.

b) The dog, a furry shark, circled the table.

c) The grass was a sea of green waves.

3 marks

2 Write a **metaphor** for each word.

a) silk _____

_____

b) orange _____

_____

2 marks

Marks.......... /5

Similes and Metaphors

Challenge 3

1 Write **S** for simile and **M** for metaphor next to each sentence.

a) The stream was a silver ribbon. ☐

b) The woodlouse was covered in armoured plates, like a tiny dinosaur. ☐

c) The clouds looked like a flock of lambs, rushing across the sky. ☐

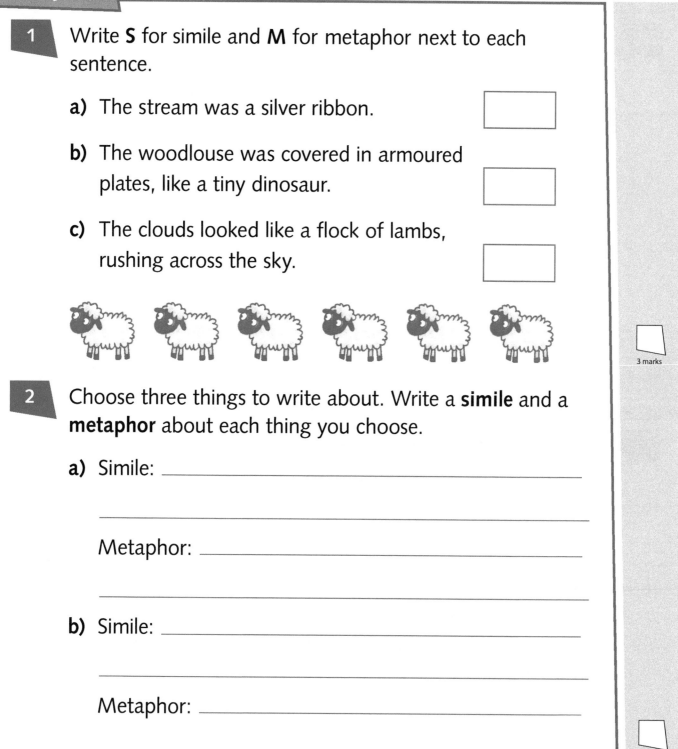

3 marks

2 Choose three things to write about. Write a **simile** and a **metaphor** about each thing you choose.

a) Simile: _____

_____

Metaphor: _____

_____

b) Simile: _____

_____

Metaphor: _____

_____

4 marks

Marks.......... /7

Total marks .... /17

How am I doing?

Story Plots and Characters

Challenge 1

1 Describe the plot of your favourite story or film. Don't forget to describe the beginning, how the story moves on, what problems are faced, how they are solved and how the story ends.

_____

_____

_____

_____

_____

5 marks

Marks.......... /5

Challenge 2

1 Choose your favourite story villain.

a) Is there something about their appearance that gives you a hint that the character is a villain?

_____

_____

b) Do the clothes that the character wears tell you that they are wicked? Does the style or colour give you a hint?

_____

_____

c) What is the character's voice like? Does anything about the voice let you know that the character is a villain?

_____

_____

3 marks

Marks.......... /3

Story Plots and Characters

Challenge 3

1 Write a plot outline of the story of a great adventure. It could be a journey to a hidden, mysterious island, or a strange planet far out in space – you choose!

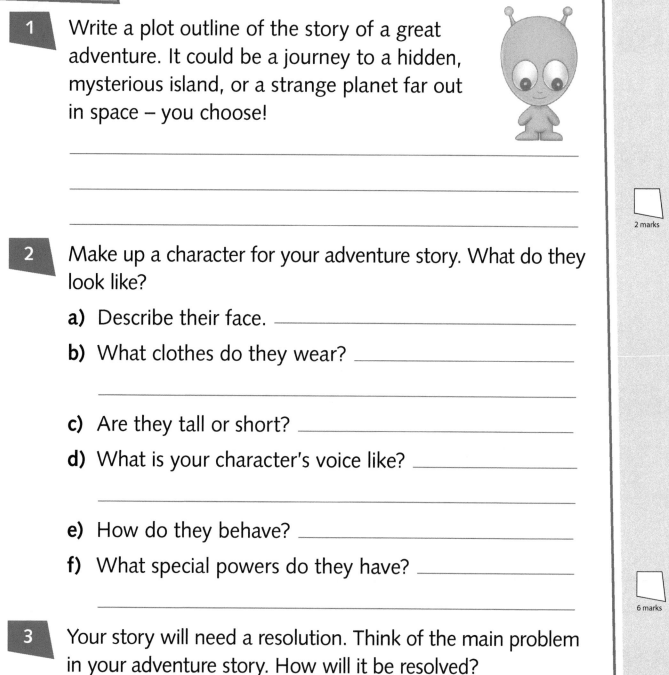

_____

_____

_____

2 marks

2 Make up a character for your adventure story. What do they look like?

a) Describe their face. _____

b) What clothes do they wear? _____

_____

c) Are they tall or short? _____

d) What is your character's voice like? _____

_____

e) How do they behave? _____

f) What special powers do they have? _____

_____

6 marks

3 Your story will need a resolution. Think of the main problem in your adventure story. How will it be resolved?

_____

_____

_____

2 marks

Marks......... /10

Total marks .... /18

How am I doing?

Does it Make Sense?

G Grammar   P Punctuation   S Spelling

Challenge 1

G **1** Read these sentences. Underline anything that does not make sense. Explain why it does not make sense.

> My dad is very tall and my mum is small but he has short hair and a beard. They like the beach. I went out there with them and saw it, but it was hot. We picked up sea glass.

_____

_____

_____

_____

3 marks

GPS **2** Be the teacher! Correct the mistakes in these sentences.

a) I cant do my werk because it is to hard.

b) We went to the beech and had sum ice creem.

c) My favourite cake is chocklit cake but
my sister likes ginjer cake best.

3 marks

Marks.......... /6

Challenge 2

G **1** Write a paragraph about your favourite animal. Read it back to check it makes sense.

_____

_____

_____

3 marks

Does it Make Sense?

GP | **2** There are three mistakes in each sentence. Find them and rewrite the sentences correctly.

a) i like cat best because they are furry

_____

_____

b) My baby brothers oliver and james are noisy

_____

_____

2 marks

Marks.......... /5

Challenge 3

G | **1** Write a paragraph about your school. Read it back to check it makes sense.

_____

_____

_____

3 marks

PS | **2** Read these instructions and correct any mistakes.

Too rap a present you need paper tape sissors and a lable. Put the present on the paper and cut it too the write size. Tape it shut and fold over the edges Make sure everything looks neet

11 marks

Marks.......... /14

Total marks .... /25   How am I doing? ☺ 😐 😖

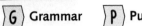 **G** Grammar   **P** Punctuation   **S** Spelling

S **1.** Try these **sp** words. Show how you would change these **sp** words into chunks to learn the spellings.

     a) space ⟶ _____ + _____

     b) spit ⟶ _____ + _____

     c) spade ⟶ _____ + _____

     d) spider ⟶ _____ + _____

4 marks

2. Write instructions for how to make a pizza.

     a) Ingredients:

     _____   _____

     _____   _____

     _____

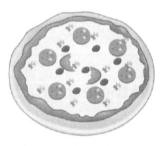

     b) Method:

     • _____

     • _____

     • _____

2 marks

P **3.** Using the pictures to help you, write a list of what each person saw at the park. Don't forget your commas!

a)

Elle saw _____

b)

Jake saw _____

c)

David saw _____

3 marks

4. Write a review of your favourite café or restaurant. What do you like best about it? What is the food like? Are the people friendly? How is the place decorated?

_____

_____

_____

2 marks

G **5.** Choose the homophone that makes sense. Draw a circle around the correct word in each sentence.

a) At **knight / night**, I sleep in my bed.

b) Will you **bee / be** ready soon?

c) Please come over **hear / here**.

d) We **ate / eight** our dinner all up.

4 marks

6. Write a simile for each thing in the list.

a) cat _____

b) water _____

c) wind _____

d) lizard _____

4 marks

7. Write a metaphor for each thing in the list.

 a) rain _____

 b) sea _____

 c) mouse _____

 d) sugar _____

4 marks

PS **8.** Proofread this paragraph and find the mistakes. Rewrite the paragraph correctly.

> I wanted two go too the woods four a walk but it
>
> was ranining. I decided too go anyway and put on my
>
> welies and my raincoat. It wasn't to wet in the end so
>
> that was good reely

_____

_____

_____

_____

9 marks

Capital Letters and Full Stops

G Grammar **P** Punctuation **S** Spelling

Challenge 1

P **1** The full stops and capital letters are missing from these sentences. Add them in the correct places.

> **Example:** Ṫhe cat ran into the garden and scared the birds.

a) the sun is so bright we need our sunglasses

b) we went to play football in the park

c) my sister likes apple juice but I prefer pineapple juice

3 marks

P **2** Write the full stops and capital letters in the correct places, just like you did in question 1.

> she saw the dog steal my sausage it sneaked up to the table
>
> and grabbed it it was really naughty now there are no sausages
>
> left the dog will have to stay in the garden at teatime

10 marks

Marks......... /13

Challenge 2

P **1** Correct these sentences by adding the full stops and capital letters.

a) the raindrops fell into the puddle with a loud plop

b) the garden is full of bugs like spiders and worms

Capital Letters and Full Stops

c) we built a model using old junk

3 marks

P **2** Draw a circle round each missing capital letter.
Add the missing full stops.

a) i saw a starfish in the rockpool

b) a mouse ran across the garden and hid in the wall

c) my friend likes playing games about space, so we do
that a lot

3 marks

Marks.......... /6

Challenge 3

P **1** Write an answer to each question. Write in full sentences
and use capital letters and full stops.

a) What colour is your hair?

_____

b) What colour are your eyes?

_____

2 marks

P **2** Write the full stops and capital letters in this paragraph.

i love making pizza for my friends i bake the base first, and then
add tomato sauce i add sliced vegetables next last of all i add
cheese and herbs before my dad helps me to bake it in the oven

9 marks

Marks.......... /11

Total marks .... /30   How am I doing? 🙂 😐 😣

Question Marks and Exclamation Marks

G Grammar   P Punctuation   S Spelling

Challenge 1

P 1   Write in the missing capital letters and exclamation marks.
Add them in the correct places.

> T
> **Example:** that noise made me jump!

a) i can't wait to see you

b) it's nearly my birthday and i could pop with excitement

c) that is too hot

3 marks

P 2   Add the missing question marks and capital letters to this
paragraph, in the same way as you did in question 1.

> do you like cats perhaps you prefer dogs do
>
> you like rabbits best do you think it is easier
>
> to have a pet that you do not need to walk
>
> every day do you know what each pet eats
>
> do you know what sort of bed they need it is
>
> important for your pet to be comfortable.

13 marks

Marks......... /16

Challenge 2

P 1   Write the missing capital letters, exclamation marks and
full stops in this paragraph.

Question Marks and Exclamation Marks

i went into my bedroom to look for my skates i looked under the bed and saw a spider scuttling towards me i don't know who was more surprised – me or the spider i screamed and my mum ran in to see what was wrong she laughed when i told her and we caught the spider and put it outside in the garden where it would be safe

11 marks

P **2** Write the missing capital letters, question marks or full stops in these sentences.

a) would you like a lolly

b) she is going to be okay

c) who wants to go to the beach

3 marks

Marks......... /14

Challenge 3

P **1** Write out three sentences. One that ends with a full stop, one with an exclamation mark and one with a question mark.

a)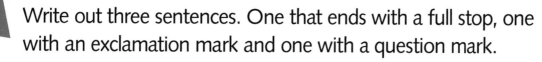

b) _____

c) _____

3 marks

Marks......... /3

Total marks .... /33

How am I doing?

Commas

 G Grammar   **P** Punctuation   **S** Spelling

Challenge 1

GP **1** Rewrite these sentences putting the commas in the lists. Remember to add an 'and' before the last item in the list.

a) Sara bought oranges apples bananas strawberries grapes at the market.

_____

_____

b) Julie had marbles string a pencil a bar of chocolate in her pocket.

_____

_____

c) At the circus I saw clowns a trapeze artist acrobats jugglers.

_____

_____

d) Collies pugs spaniels huskies are all breeds of dog.

_____

_____

4 marks

Marks.......... /4

Challenge 2

GP **1** Rewrite these sentences putting commas in the lists and adding an 'and'.

a) I have dolls trains teddies puzzles in my toy box.

_____

_____

Commas

b) We need to feed the dogs cats rabbits guinea pigs.

_____

_____

c) In my paint box there are red green yellow white blue black paints.

_____

_____

d) Don't forget to bring your lunch notebook pens coat on the trip.

_____

_____

4 marks

Marks.......... /4

Challenge 3

GP 1 Write these words as a list in a sentence:

a) | cake | bread | scones | buns |

_____

_____

b) | red | pink | purple | white | brown |

_____

_____

c) | monkeys | elephants | bears | tigers | lions |

_____

_____

3 marks

Marks.......... /3

Total marks .... /11   How am I doing?   ☺ 😐 ☹

Present Tense

Challenge 1

G **1** Circle the word in each pair that is in the present tense.

a) walked / walk

b) shout / shouted

c) jump / jumped

3 marks

G **2** Underline the word in each pair that is in the present tense.

a) fly / flew

b) smile / smiled

c) laugh / laughed

3 marks

Marks......... /6

Challenge 2

G **1** Choose the correct word for each sentence from the box, and write it in the space.

skipping   ate   skipped   eating   barks   barking

a) I am _____ in the sun.

b) I love _____ strawberries.

c) My dog _____ all day.

3 marks

Present Tense

2 Draw lines to match the words to complete the following sentences.

I love	shining.
The sun is	swimming.
It is	snowing.

3 marks

Marks.......... /6

Challenge 3

6 **1** Rewrite the underlined actions in the present tense.

a) The snow <u>sparkled</u>.

The snow is _____.

b) I <u>dropped</u> a plate.

I am _____ a plate.

c) I am <u>slid</u> down the hill.

I am _____ down the hill.

3 marks

6 **2** Underline the correct word in each sentence.

a) The wind is **blew / blowing**.

b) My cat is **purring / purred** so loud right now that I can't sleep!

c) The mouse is **ran / running** quickly so the cat cannot catch her.

3 marks

Marks.......... /6

Total marks .... /18

How am I doing?

Past Tense

G Grammar   P Punctuation   S Spelling

G 1 Change these sentences to the past tense to make new sentences.

a) The wind **is blowing** hard today!

The wind _____ hard yesterday!

b) There **are** three rabbits in the garden.

Yesterday, there _____ three rabbits in the garden.

c) Suki **is** drinking orange juice today.

Yesterday, Suki _____ drinking orange juice.

3 marks

G 2 Match the words to the correct past tense using a line.

smile	ran
look	looked
run	smiled

3 marks

Marks.......... /6

G 1 Complete these sentences so that they make sense. Remember to use the correct tense.

a) Today I _____.

b) Yesterday I _____.

c) Today I _____

but yesterday I _____.

3 marks

Past Tense

2 Write the past tense version of each verb.

a) cry   ⟶ _____

b) shriek ⟶ _____

c) walk   ⟶ _____

3 marks

Marks.......... /6

Challenge 3

1 Add **–ed** to these verbs to change them from the present tense to the past tense.

a) laugh ⟶ _____

b) sew   ⟶ _____

c) plant ⟶ _____

3 marks

2 Change these verbs from the present tense to the past tense.

a) swim ⟶ _____

b) run   ⟶ _____

c) sing   ⟶ _____

3 marks

Marks.......... /6

Total marks .... /18   How am I doing?

Apostrophes

G Grammar **P** Punctuation **S** Spelling

Challenge 1

P **1** Add the possessive apostrophes to these plural nouns.

a) The h o r s e s saddles are grey.

b) The g i r l s bags are heavy.

c) The c a t s toys were fluffy.

d) The s i n g e r s dressing rooms were cold.

e) The t e a c h e r s cars were all covered in snow.

f) The b o y s coats are black.

6 marks

P **2** Circle the words with contractions in each list.

a) couldn't   could   would

b) did   didn't   do

c) isn't   is   are

3 marks

Marks.......... /9

Challenge 2

P **1** Add **'s** to make these plural nouns possessive.

a) children_____ b) women_____ c) men_____

3 marks

P **2** Change the words to their contractions. Write the contractions in the spaces.

a) will not ⟶ _____

b) can not ⟶ _____

c) I would ⟶ _____

3 marks

Marks.......... /6

Challenge 3

G | **1** Underline the correct plural in each sentence.

a) The **doctors' / doctors's** coats are white.

b) The **houses' / houses's** doors are all green.

c) The **farmers' / farmers's** sheep are fluffy.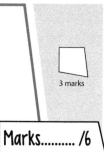

d) The **women's / womens's** nails are long.

e) The **men's / mens's** cars are silver.

f) The **children's / childrens's** T-shirts are too big.

6 marks

P | **2** Write a contraction in each sentence.

a) I _____ get the door open.

b) _____ like that.

c) _____ the best football player in school.

d) They _____ win the match, but they came very close.

e) They had better hurry up, _____ not got much time left!

f) _____ leave the cakes in the oven too long – they will burn!

6 marks

Marks.......... /12

Total marks .... /27   How am I doing?

Conjunctions

G) Grammar   P) Punctuation   S) Spelling

Challenge 1

GP | 1 Use the conjunction **and** to make each set of two sentences into one. Don't forget to change the capital letters too!

a) My dog has bad breath. He needs his nails trimmed.

_____

b) My favourite cake is chocolate flavour. My favourite drink is orange squash.

_____

2 marks

GP | 2 Use the conjunction **when** to make each set of two sentences into one. Don't forget to change the capital letters too!

a) Kassy can go to the park. Her class is over.

_____

b) I will go to the beach. It is a sunny day.

_____

2 marks

Marks.......... /4

Challenge 2

G | 1 Use **or** to make each set of two sentences into one. Don't forget to change the capital letters too!

a) Should I stay at home? Should I go out?

_____

b) I could wear a dress. I could wear a skirt.

_____

2 marks

Conjunctions

G **2** Use **because** to make each set of two sentences into one. Don't forget to change the capital letters too!

a) Tom has a stomach ache. He ate too much ice cream.

_____

b) I opened the window. It was hot.

_____

2 marks

Marks.......... /4

Challenge 3

G **1** Write three sentences that use **but** to join ideas.

> **Example:** I have new shoes **but** I don't have a new coat.

a) _____

b) _____

c) _____

3 marks

G **2** Write three sentences that use **if** to join ideas

> **Example:** Those flowers will bloom soon **if** the sun keeps shining.

a) _____

b) _____

c) _____

3 marks

Marks.......... /6

Total marks .... /14

How am I doing?

Nouns, Noun Phrases and Adjectives

G Grammar   **P** Punctuation   **S** Spelling

Challenge 1

G **1** Circle the common nouns in each list of words.

a) dogs   and   monkeys   this   taken

b) mouse   from   onion   badger   the

c) girl   go   trace   table   ladybird

3 marks

G **2** Underline the noun phrases.

a) The cat meowed.   b) The woman smiled.

2 marks

G **3** Circle the adjective in each sentence.

a) The rough waves rushed up the beach.

b) The fluffy cat jumped off the wall.

2 marks

Marks.........../7

Challenge 2

G **1** Tick the proper nouns in each set.

a) mouse ☐   Brighton ☐   leaf ☐   England ☐

b) glass ☐   Italy ☐   beach ☐   Raj ☐

c) book ☐   page ☐   heart ☐   Marie ☐

3 marks

G **2** Fill the blanks to expand the noun phrases.

> **Example:** The creepy man, with white hair.

a) The _____ house, with _____.

b) The _____ creature, with _____.

c) The _____ cat, with _____.

3 marks

Nouns, Noun Phrases and Adjectives

G **3** Write an adjective for each sentence.

a) The _____ rain soaked my coat.

b) The _____ butterfly landed on a flower.

c) The girl plaited her _____ hair.

3 marks

Marks.......... /9

Challenge 3

G **1** Write **C** next to the common nouns and **P** next to the proper nouns.

a) Kate ☐   b) bird ☐   c) India ☐

3 marks

G **2** Pick three nouns from the box and use them to write expanded noun phrases.

| rabbit | boat | window | lake | fox | moon |

a) _____

b) _____

c) _____

3 marks

G **3** Add an adjective to each space in the sentences.

a) The _____ fox ran into the _____ woods.

b) The _____ woman ran into the _____ house.

4 marks

Marks......... /10

Total marks .... /26   How am I doing?   ☺ 😐 ☹

105

Verbs and Adverbs

G Grammar   **P** Punctuation   **S** Spelling

G **1** Underline the verbs in each list.

a) run, chalk, bird, laugh

b) elephant, sit, paper, jump

c) twig, rose, sleep, leap

3 marks

G **2** Circle the adverb that describes the underlined verb.

a) The girl <u>shouted</u> loudly.

b) Dave <u>left</u> early.

c) The dog <u>came</u> here when it was called.

3 marks

Marks.......... /6

G **1** Choose a verb from the box for each sentence.

| waved | burned | ate | chased | carried | fluttered |

a) My cat _____ the bird.

b) A man _____ the bag up the stairs.

c) The flag _____ in the breeze.

d) The man _____ the fly away from his face.

e) A mouse _____ the cheese.

f) The fire _____ brightly.

6 marks

G **2** Choose an adverb from the box that fits each sentence, and write it in the space. You will not use them all.

| softly | brightly | silently | angrily | sadly |

Verbs and Adverbs

a) The fireworks flashed _____ in the sky.

b) The snake slithered _____ across the grass.

c) The water lapped _____ across the sand.

3 marks

Marks.......... /9

Challenge 3

G | **1** Write a verb to complete each sentence.

a) The dog _____ on the bed.

b) The girl _____ in the garden.

c) The snail _____ up the wall.

3 marks

G | **2** Write two sentences of your own. Underline the verb in each sentence.

a) _____

b) _____

2 marks

G | **3** Write an adverb at the end of each sentence.

a) I ran along the road _____.

b) I ate the sandwich _____.

c) I held the hamster _____.

3 marks

G | **4** Write two sentences containing an adverb. Underline each adverb.

a) _____

_____

b) _____

_____

2 marks

Marks.......... /10

Total marks .... /25   How am I doing?

1. Imagine you are teaching a Reception class to draw a picture. Write instructions to explain how to draw a picture of a tree, with flowers and an animal on the grass.

_____

_____

_____

2 marks

P 2. Add the possessive apostrophes to the words in red.

   a) The b a b y s eyes were green.

   b) The g i r l s hat was purple.

   c) The d o g s tail wagged as she ate her bone.

3 marks

P 3. Add the missing exclamation marks and capital letters to these paragraphs.

   a) it went bang it was really loud i love
   fireworks they made the baby cry though
   they were so pretty i jumped when the last
   one went off it was so loud

   b) that really hurt i wish you hadn't stepped
   on me you should look where you are
   going it hurt so much

c)

> don't do that it's really mean i wish you would think about things before you do them it was so silly

3 marks

[G] **4.** Circle the adjective in each pair.

a) 　dog　　　　pink

b) 　fabric　　　glittery

c) 　tiny　　　　bag

d) 　massive　　peg

e) 　ancient　　man

5 marks

[G] **5.** Underline the adjective in each sentence.

a) The smooth pebble rolled down the hill.

b) The juicy pineapple squirted my face!

c) The tiny mouse scuttled under the chair.

d) My old jumper fell apart.

4 marks

G Grammar   P Punctuation   S Spelling

6. Write down your memories of your best birthday ever.
What was so great about it?

_____

_____

_____

_____

4 marks

G **7.** Here are five adverbs. Choose one that fits each sentence and write it in the space.

brightly   lazily   noisily   slowly   quickly

a) The hedgehog snuffled _____.

b) The crab ran _____ across the sand.

c) The gem glittered _____ in the sunshine.

d) The slug slithered _____ up the wall.

e) The mermaid sat _____ on a rock, watching the shore.

5 marks

6   **8.** Circle the correct possessive plural in each sentence.

    a) The **teachers' / teachers's** books are heavy.

    b) The **farmers' / farmers's** chickens are noisy!

    c) The **women's / womens's** watches are new.

    d) The **men's / mens's** shoes are big.

    e) The **children's / childrens's** ice lollies are sticky.

5 marks

P   **9.** Change these words to contractions.

    a) will not   ⟶   _____

    b) shall not   ⟶   _____

    c) can not   ⟶   _____

    d) is not   ⟶   _____

    e) I am   ⟶   _____

5 marks

Marks........ /36

Notes

Answers

Pages 4–11
Starter Test
1. a) Mo n d a y
   b) T u e s d ay
   c) W ednes d a y
   d) Th u r s d a y
   e) F r i d a y
   f) S at u r d a y
   g) Su n d a y
2. a) jkl m n o pq
   b) cde f g h ijk
   c) ij k l m n opq
   d) rst u v w xyz
   e) tuv w x y z
3. a) undone
   b) uncooked
   c) unfair
   d) untied
4. Make sure your child has written the letters neatly.
   a) ABCD
   b) EFGH
   c) IJKL
   d) MNOP
   e) QRST
   f) UVW
   g) XYZ
5. a) **T**he lady sat on the chair.
   b) **T**he horse jumped over the fence.
   c) **T**he hedgehog slept in the leaves.
   d) **T**he bath filled with bubbles.
6. a) **L**ondon
   b) **T**uesday
   c) **S**ue
   d) **R**ajan
   e) **R**ome
   f) **S**aturday
7. a) It's cold!
   b) That's nasty!
   c) How rude!
   d) How awful!
   e) That's so smelly!
8. a) What's the time?
   b) Can I come?
   c) What's your name?
   d) Do you like ice cream?
   e) What's that sound?
9. a) ra/bbit
   b) tor/toise
   c) kan/ga/roo
   d) li/on
   e) ti/ger

10. a) pitch
    b) patch
    c) hutch
    d) fetch
    e) kitchen
11. a) catch**er**
    b) pitch**er**
    c) sharp**er**
    d) small**er**
    e) tall**er**
12. a) cold**est**
    b) straight**est**
    c) loud**est**
    d) bright**est**
13. a) ha**ve**
    b) lo**ve**
    c) li**ve**
    d) glo**ve**
    e) gi**ve**
14. a) flu**ff**
    b) sta**ff**
    c) stu**ff**
    d) cu**ff**
    e) blu**ff**
15. a) fu**ss**
    b) me**ss**
    c) pre**ss**
    d) cre**ss**
    e) stre**ss**
16. a) fu**zz**
    b) bu**zz**
    c) mu**zz**le
    d) nu**zz**le
    e) pu**zz**le
17. a) butterflies
    b) rattlesnake
    c) himself
    d) grasshopper
    e) basketball
    f) fireworks
    g) airport
    h) skateboard

Pages 12–13
Challenge 1
1. 5 marks: talking to a friend about their favourite TV show, listening carefully to what they say, responding appropriately, engaging in conversation, remembering what they said. All present for 5 marks; four correct for 4 marks; three correct for 3 marks, two correct for 2 marks, one correct for 1 mark.

Answers

2. 5 marks: talking to a grown up about their childhood games, asking relevant questions, listening carefully to the answers, responding appropriately, engaging in conversation. All present for 5 marks; four correct for 4 marks; three correct for 3 marks, two correct for 2 marks, one correct for 1 mark.

Challenge 2
1. 5 marks: asking questions relevant to the task, listening to the answers, writing down the instructions in order, including all the instructions needed, following the instructions to make the model. All present for 5 marks; four correct for 4 marks; three correct for 3 marks, two correct for 2 marks, one correct for 1 mark.
2. 5 marks: asking a grown up relevant questions, listening carefully to the answers, responding appropriately, engaging in conversation, remembering what they said. All present for 5 marks; four correct for 4 marks; three correct for 3 marks, two correct for 2 marks, one correct for 1 mark.

Challenge 3
1. 5 marks: asking five relevant questions about an exhibit. 1 mark per relevant question.
2. 5 marks: thinking of a particular subject, asking a librarian to help, asking several relevant questions, listening carefully to the answers, responding appropriately. All present for 5 marks; four correct for 4 marks; three correct for 3 marks, two correct for 2 marks, one correct for 1 mark.

Pages 14–15
Challenge 1
1. A mark should be given for each of the things noted that is successfully described.
2. A mark should be given for each of the things noted that is successfully explained.

Challenge 2
1. A mark should be given for each of the things noted that is successfully described.
2. A mark should be given for each of the things noted that is successfully explained.

Challenge 3
1. A mark should be given for each of the things noted that is successfully described.
2. A mark should be given for each of the things noted that is successfully explained.

Pages 16–17
Challenge 1
1. A mark should be given for each of the things noted that is successfully described.
2. A mark should be given for each of the things noted that is successfully described.

Challenge 2
1. Award marks for an ordered narrative – it should be in sequence and make sense.
2. Award marks for an ordered narrative – it should be in sequence and make sense.

Challenge 3
1. Award marks for an ordered narrative – it should be in sequence and make sense.
2. Award marks for an ordered narrative – it should be in sequence and make sense.

Pages 18–19
Challenge 1
1. Listen to your child and take notice of what they say.
   Award up to 5 points for their presentation.
2. Listen to your child and take notice of what they say.
   Award up to 5 points for their presentation.

Challenge 2
1. Listen to your child and take notice of what they say.
   Award up to 5 points for their presentation.
2. Listen to your child and take notice of what they say.
   Award up to 5 points for their presentation.

Challenge 3
1. Listen to your child and take notice of what they say.
   Award up to 5 points for their role-play.
2. Listen to your child and take notice of what they say.
   Award up to 5 points for their presentation.

Pages 20–21
Challenge 1
1. a) blue, black
   b) blade, blood
   c) blend, bleat
2. a) stamp, stink
   b) must, fast, master, mist
   c) last, test

Challenge 2
1. a) drip, drink
   b) drill, drum
   c) dress, drop

2. **a)** graph, elephant
   b) phrase, photo
   c) phone, phantom

Challenge 3
1. **a)** those, bath
   b) that, these
   c) path, then
2. **a)** growl, grape
   b) grind
   c) grate, grab

Pages 22–23
Challenge 1
1. **a)** strawberry
   b) postcard
   c) lighthouse
2. **a)** tablecloth   **b)** crossroads
   c) toothache

Challenge 2
1. **a)** football   **b)** footpath
   c) armchair
2. **a)** Any correct compound word
   b) Any correct compound word
   c) Any correct compound word

Challenge 3
1. **a)** paintbrush = **paint** + **brush** so 'paintbrush' means a brush for painting.
   b) rainbow = **rain** + **bow** so 'rainbow' means a bow shape, formed when both rain and sunny weather happen together.
   c) handmade = **hand** + **made** so 'handmade' means made by hand.
2. **a)** From the sun. Solar power is power generated by the sun, for example.
   b) Temperature meter; describes how warm or cool the temperature is.
   c) Empty space, with nothing in it at all - not even air!

Pages 24–25
Challenge 1
1. **a)** chain, paint
   b) stain, faint
   c) pain, rain
2. **a)** feet
   b) seen
   c) deep

Challenge 2
1. **a)** Any sentence containing the word 'believe' used correctly.

b) Any sentence containing the word 'field' used correctly.
c) Any sentence containing the word 'shriek' used correctly.
2. Make sure your child knows what each word means.
   a) deceive ✓
   b) receipt ✓
   c) receive ✓

Challenge 3
1. **a)** Any sentence containing the word 'survey' used correctly.
   b) Any sentence containing the word 'maybe' used correctly.
   c) Any sentence containing the word 'stain' used correctly.
2. **a)** Any sentence containing a word with the grapheme 'ie' used correctly.
   b) Any sentence containing a word with the grapheme 'ee' used correctly.
   c) Any sentence containing a word with the grapheme 'ea' used correctly.

Pages 26–27
Challenge 1
1. **a)** won't   **b)** can't   **c)** don't
2.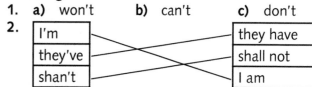

Challenge 2
1. **a)** won't   **b)** can't   **c)** I'm
2. **a)** won't   **b)** she'll   **c)** I'm

Challenge 3
1. **a)** wouldn't
   b) I'm
   c) don't
2. **I'd** like a cat, but my mum **won't** let me. **She's** got an allergy to cat hair. I **can't** have a dog because we live in a small flat so **I've** asked if I can have a hamster instead.

Pages 28–29
Challenge 1
1.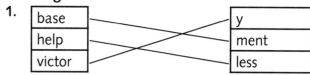

Answers

2.

life		ful
help		able
comfort		like

Challenge 2
1. a) messed up; not neatly made
   b) take again
   c) rude
2. a) not like
   b) amazing; hard to believe
   c) a new version

Challenge 3
1. a) amaze**ment**
   b) dry**ness**
   c) sad**ness**
2. a) Any appropriate root word. For example: payment, tournament, excitement.
   b) Any appropriate root word. For example: armful, blissful, bucketful.
   c) Any appropriate root word. For example: redness, blindness, goodness.

Pages 30–31
Challenge 1
1. a) Any choice of the words 'leathery', 'scaly', 'furry', 'spiny', with a suitable explanation.
   b) Any choice of the words 'bubbly', 'fizzy', 'foamy', 'fluffy', with a suitable explanation.
   c) Any choice of the words 'giggle', 'howl', 'laugh', 'squeak', with a suitable explanation.
2. Three phrases underlined. Can your child explain why they have chosen particular phrases?

Challenge 2
1. a) Any choice from the words 'The dragon roared and spit fire into the darkness of the cave', with a suitable explanation.
   b) Any choice from the words 'The spider slid down a thread of silk, and dangled in the breeze', with a suitable explanation.
   c) Any choice from the words 'The juice poured down my chin, as I crunched the shiny green apple', with a suitable explanation.
2. 3 marks: 1 mark for two favourite phrases underlined, 2 further marks for explaining why each one was chosen.

Challenge 3
1. The child should keep a notebook filled with their favourite words and phrases, to help them learn and spell new words correctly.

Pages 32–33
Challenge 1
1.

Challenge 2
1. 6 marks: 1 mark per section of the story re-told correctly.

Challenge 3
1. 5 marks: the 5 main events must be covered and retold through the wicked queen's eyes.
   For example: I ordered the huntsman to kill Snow White because she was prettier than me.
   I discovered that the huntsman did not kill her after all. I poisoned an apple and went to the Seven Dwarves' cottage. Snow White bit the apple and died. The handsome prince kissed her and she woke.
   All present for 5 marks; four correct for 4 marks; three correct for 3 marks, two correct for 2 marks, one correct for 1 mark.

Pages 34–35
Challenge 1
1. a) Any fiction book of the child's choice.
   b) Because the story is made up.
   c) Fiction is a made-up story; non-fiction is facts.

Challenge 2

1. **a)** Any answer explaining why the child does or doesn't enjoy reading non-fiction.
   b) A description of any feature, such as fact boxes, the child has chosen from a non-fiction book.
   c) The child's favourite non-fiction book, with an explanation as to why they chose this book.

Challenge 3

1. **a)** The book must be a story that features new technology or is set in the future.
   b) No, not always.
   c) The title of any science fiction book suitable for children – such as *The Iron Man* by Ted Hughes

2. **a)** Any humorous story the child has read and why they found it funny.
   b) An explanation of why they knew it was a comedy.
   c) The name of any two humorous books or series – such as *Too Ghoul for School* by B. Strange or *Horrid Henry* by Francesca Simon. A quick look in any library or bookshop will reveal many more!

Pages 36–37

Challenge 1

1. **a)** crabs, tiny insects, winkles and shellfish
   b) Any three from the following: crab shells, empty shells, cuttlefish bones and feathers.
   c) Fishing line and plastic bottles.

Challenge 2

1. **a)** Any four from the following: red, orange, yellow, green, blue, indigo and violet.
   b) When it rains and is sunny at the same time.
   c) Richard Of York Gave Battle In Vain.

Challenge 3

1. **a)** Animals that are awake at night.
   b) Any three from the following: bats, hedgehogs, badgers and owls.
   c) Wildlife wardens and animal charities.

Pages 38–39

Challenge 1

1. **a)** a spaceman   **b)** a bowl
   c) an alien

Challenge 2

1. **a)** garden
   b) mouse
   c) shiny red berry

Challenge 3

1. **a)** A pirate
   b) Big gold earrings and a striped jersey
   c) Sail, fight sea serpents and find buried treasure

Pages 40–41

Challenge 1

1. **a)** Sad
   b) Trudged and dragging
   c) He had been laughed at.

Challenge 2

1. **a)** Snowflakes
   b) She hadn't seen snow before.
   c) Winter

Challenge 3

1. **a)** To a theme park.
   b) The child says they have been begging and dreaming. It also says 'I couldn't believe we were going after all this time.'
   c) Any suitable answer, for example: happy, excited.

Pages 42–43

Challenge 1

1. **a)** It tells a story.
   b) Rhyme
   c) motion and ocean

Challenge 2

1. **a)** A concrete poem.
   b) A poem written in a shape.
   c) Any appropriate shape. For example: a leaf, a tree.

Challenge 3

1. **a)** Any suitable made-up words.
   b) Any suitable made-up words.
   c) Any suitable made-up words.
   d) Any suitable nonsense poem.

Pages 44–45

Challenge 1

1. **a)** Pickle
   b) Salad
   c) A knife

Challenge 2

1. **a)** emerald
   b) topaz
   c) garnet

Challenge 3

1. **a)** Old packaging
   b) Big circles cut from card or paper
   c) A triangle

Answers

Pages 46–47
Challenge 1
1. a) Grandma   b) A dibber
    c) Carrot, broccoli and cauliflower seeds
Challenge 2
1. a) Alex and Leigh are going for a walk by the river.
    b) The puppies like to see ducks and geese.
    c) Daisy rolled in mud.
Challenge 3
1. a) Four oranges   b) Cloth
    c) Six apples

Pages 48–51
Progress Test 1
1. 2 marks: ask a friend at least two questions about their favourite film, write down their answers. All present for 2 marks; one correct for 1 mark.
2. 2 marks: at least two valid reasons given for why the child likes a particular toy or game. Both present for 2 marks; one correct for 1 mark.
3. 2 marks: at least two valid memories of the holiday or day out. Both present for 2 marks; one correct for 1 mark.
4. 2 marks: at least two valid and explained opinions on the topic. Both present for 2 marks; one correct for 1 mark.
5. a) The dog's ears are floppy.
    b) The boy's teddy was brown.
    c) The woman's hair was blonde.
6. 4 marks: the 4 main events must be covered and retold through a reporter's eyes. For example: The king orders the miller's daughter to spin straw into gold and a dwarf does it for her in return for her necklace and her ring; the next day the dwarf spins a bigger pile of straw into gold in return for the girl's first born child; years later the girl has a baby and begs the dwarf not to take it which he agrees to, as long as the girl can guess his name; the girl guesses the dwarf's name correctly – Rumpelstiltskin. All present for 4 marks; three correct for 3 marks, two correct for 2 marks, one correct for 1 mark.
7. a) A special material made from chewed-up wood.
    b) Saliva
    c) The queen
    d) The roof space of a house, a beam in a shed or garage.
8. a) Icing sugar, water, food colouring, and peppermint essence
    b) Peppermint essence
    c) Form the dough into a lump.
    d) Green sprinkles.

Pages 52–53
Challenge 1
1. There are no 'right' answers but here are some suggestions. Listen to your child and see if their answer is sensible.
    a) f + uss   b) cl + ass
    c) str + ess
2. a) p + er + ch   b) ch + ur + ch
    c) mu + ch
Challenge 2
1. a) cr + isp   b) wa + sp
    c) spi + der
2. a) st + and   b) fa + st
    c) wa + ste
Challenge 3
1. a) th + ump
    b) m + oth
    c) fif + th
2. a) whi + zz
    b) fi + zz
    c) bu + zz

Pages 54–55
Challenge 1
1. a) ta / ble
    b) pa / per
    c) smi / ling
2. a) ba / by
    b) don / key
    c) ra / bbit
Challenge 2
1. a) an / i / mal
    b) di / no / saur
    c) pel / i / can
2. a) Sep / tem / ber
    b) Oct / o / ber
    c) No / vem / ber
Challenge 3
1. telephone   Saturday   radio
2. a) 3   b) 2   c) 1

Pages 56–57
Challenge 1
1. a) night   b) night
    c) knight   d) knight

2. **a)** bee   **b)** be
    c) be   **d)** Be

Challenge 2
1. **a)** They're   **b)** their
    c) there   **d)** their
2. **a)** sea   **b)** see
    c) sea   **d)** See

Challenge 3
1. **a)** tale   **b)** tail
    c) tail   **d)** tale
2. **a)** except   **b)** accept
    c) except   **d)** accept

Pages 58–59
Challenge 1
1. **a)** gnat
    b) gnome
    c) knit
    d) knot
2. **a)** wrong
    b) wrote
    c) wriggle

Challenge 2
1. **a)** knitted
    b) gnat
    c) knight
    d) knot
2. Can your child spell the words correctly when tested?

Challenge 3
1. The (gnat) and the dragonfly flew over the pond. A (knot) of grass hung over the edge of the water, next to a (gnome). The (gnat) flew close to a butterfly and (knocked) into her wing. "Sorry!" he called.
2. wring   wrong

Pages 60–61
Challenge 1
1. **a)** bridge
    b) page
    c) wedge
2. **a)** countries
    b) babies
    c) memories
3. **a)** tickle
    b) apple
    c) castle

Challenge 2
1. **a)–c)** Check that your child can spell the words when tested.
2. **a)** valley   **b)** survey   **c)** monkey

3.
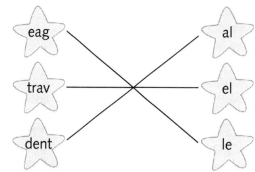

Challenge 3
1. **a)** lollies
    b) holidays
    c) keys
3. **a)** table
    b) towel
    c) total

Pages 62–63
Challenge 1
1. **a)** Any suitable sentence using 'cold'. For example: I drank a cold drink.
    b) Any suitable sentence using 'gold'. For example: My mum has a gold ring.
    c) Any suitable sentence using 'fold'. For example: Fold the paper in half.
2. **a)** Any suitable sentence using 'last'. For example: I ate a cake last night.
    b) Any suitable sentence using 'past'. For example: The birds flew past the window.
    c) Any suitable sentence using 'father'. For example: My father likes music.

Challenge 2
1. **a)** fixing (the last consonant 'x' does not double)
    b) mixing (the last consonant 'x' does not double)
    c) boxing (the last consonant 'x' does not double)
2. **a)** Any suitable sentence using 'pretty', 'everybody' and 'grass'. For example: Everybody sat on the grass in the pretty garden.
    b) Any suitable sentence using 'class', 'plant' and 'water'. For example: The class took it in turns to water the plant.
    c) Any suitable sentence using 'break', 'move' and 'parents'. For example: My parents tried not to break the vase in the house move.

Answers

Challenge 3
1. a) because
    b) sugar
    c) clothes
2. a) A suitable mnemonic for 'every'. For example: Every Vole Eats Real Yoghurt.
    b) A suitable mnemonic for 'whole'. For example: Whales Have Only Little Ears.
    c) A suitable mnemonic for 'beautiful'. For example: Bendy Eels Always Use Ties In Five Ugly Loops.

Page 64–65
Challenge 1
1. a)–c) A neatly copied set of letters.
2. a) Line of lower case '*m*'.
    b) Line of lower case '*g*'.
    c) Line of lower case '*r*'.
3. a) Line of upper case '*D*'.
    b) Line of upper case '*X*'.
    c) Line of upper case '*Y*'.
Challenge 2
1. a)–c) A neatly copied word
2. a)–c) A neatly copied word
Challenge 3
1. a)–f) Neatly copied words and correctly spaced.
2. a)–c) Names written neatly with the letters the correct size.

Pages 66–67
Challenge 1
1. a)–c) A neatly copied word
2. a)–c) A neatly copied pattern
Challenge 2
1. a)–c) A neatly copied word
2. a)–c) A neatly copied pattern
Challenge 3
1. a)–f) A neatly copied word
2. a)–f) A neatly copied pattern

Pages 68–71
Progress Test 2
1. Any sensible suggestion; some suggestions have been given.
    a) ch + ase
    b) ch + icken
    c) ch + irp
    d) pin + ch
2. a)–d) Award one mark for each favourite word successfully explained.
3. a) I want to come (too).
    b) I saw a (bear) at the zoo.

c) (There) was a mouse in the kitchen!
d) Look over (there)!
e) (They're) best friends with my brother.
4. a) The lion's teeth are enormous.
    b) The girl's trainers are very muddy.
    c) The children's books are stacked neatly.
5. a) My favourite sweetie is **fudge**.
    b) There was **sludge** in the bottom of the bath.
    c) I **dodged** the ball as it shot towards me!
    d) I like using my **sledge** in the snow.
    e) The food was really **stodgy**.
6. a) babies
    b) candies
    c) fairies
    d) diaries
7. a) 'or' written in cursive writing.
    b) 'ot' written in cursive writing.
    c) 'mag' written in cursive writing.
    d) 'eer' written in cursive writing.
8. a) tom / a / to
    b) all / i / ga / tor
    c) ter / ri / fied
    d) wa / ter / fall
    e) esc / a / la / tor

Pages 72–73
Challenge 1
1. Appropriate game and set of five instructions in the correct order.
2. a) I like apples, oranges, bananas and satsumas.
    b) I bought a hat, socks, hankies and gloves.
    c) The dog chased pigeons, crows, seagulls and starlings.
Challenge 2
1. a) Jane bought carrots, potatoes, grapes and apples.
    b) Leon bought a toy car, a toy train, a teddy and a doll.
2. An appropriate letter from the child to a new pen pal, telling them all about their family and the town where they live, using the proper layout.
Challenge 3
1. A set of step-by-step instructions on how to make a model animal. It can be made of any material, but must include clear instructions.
2. An appropriate letter to the local newspaper, recounting something exciting seen in the child's town, using the proper layout.

Pages 74–75

Challenge 1
1. 5 marks: the child describes what happened on the family outing, where they went, who they were with, what they did, whether they had special food. All present for 5 marks; four correct for 4 marks; three correct for 3 marks, two correct for 2 marks, one correct for 1 mark.

Challenge 2
1. 5 marks: a written report of a relevant experiment, what equipment was used, an ordered method, whether it went well, what the results were. All present for 5 marks; four correct for 4 marks; three correct for 3 marks, two correct for 2 marks, one correct for 1 mark.

Challenge 3
1. 5 marks: a written report of a relevant celebration or festival, what parades or parties they saw, the decorations, whether there was any special food or clothing, what gifts were given. All present for 5 marks; four correct for 4 marks; three correct for 3 marks, two correct for 2 marks, one correct for 1 mark.

Pages 76–77

Challenge 1
1. Humpty Dumpty sat on the <u>wall</u>,
   Humpty Dumpty had a great <u>fall</u>.
   All the king's horses and all the king's <u>men</u>,
   Couldn't put Humpty together <u>again</u>.
2. A short poem where lines one and two end in a word that rhymes, and lines three and four end in a word that rhymes.

Challenge 2
1. Any monster-related words.
2. a) Wherever the child would like the monster to live, with a description.
   b) A description of the monster's personality and how the child knows.
   c) A description of anything the monster might eat.
3. 10 marks: award up to 8 marks for 'wow' words and for good use of adjectives and descriptions; award up to 2 marks for a well written and well presented poem.

Challenge 3
1. A completed poem with appropriate descriptive words in the blank spaces.
2. A completed poem with appropriate descriptive words in the blank spaces.

Pages 78–79

Challenge 1
1. 6 marks: a story plan including the setting, the main characters, the story opening, the build up, the main events, the conclusion. All present for 6 marks; five correct for 5 marks; four correct for 4 marks; three correct for 3 marks, two correct for 2 marks, one correct for 1 mark.

Challenge 2
1. 3 marks: a drawn setting with a written description of where the story is set including what the landscape is like, whether there are any buildings, what the weather is like. All present for 3 marks; two correct for 2 marks, one correct for 1 mark.

Challenge 3
1. Suitable detailed descriptions of the animals in the magical world described in Challenges 1 and 2.
2. A completed character planning chart for the main character described in Challenges 1 and 2.

Pages 80–81

Challenge 1
1. a) The caterpillar was <u>as green as a lettuce leaf</u>.
   b) The sun was <u>as yellow as a sunflower</u>.
   c) The moon looked <u>like a silver coin</u>.
2. a) Any suitable simile for 'ice'.
   b) Any suitable simile for 'slug'.

Challenge 2
1. a) The stars <u>were glitter</u>, thrown across the sky.
   b) The dog, <u>a furry shark</u>, circled the table.
   c) The grass <u>was a sea of green waves</u>.
2. a) Any suitable metaphor for 'silk'.
   b) Any suitable metaphor for 'orange'.

Challenge 3
1. a) M
   b) S
   c) S
2. a) Any suitable simile and metaphor.
   b) Any suitable simile and metaphor.

Pages 82–83

Challenge 1
1. 5 marks: a written description of a plot including the beginning, how the story moves on, problems faced, how they are solved, how the story ends. All present for 5 marks; four correct for 4 marks; three correct for 3 marks, two correct for 2 marks, one correct for 1 mark.

Answers

Challenge 2
1. **a)** A description of how the villain's appearance gives clues to their character.
   b) A description of how the villain's clothes give clues to their character.
   c) A description of how the villain's voice gives clues to their character.

Challenge 3
1. 5 marks: a plot outline of an adventure story including the beginning, how the story moves on, problems faced, how they are solved, how the story ends. All present for 5 marks; four correct for 4 marks; three correct for 3 marks, two correct for 2 marks, one correct for 1 mark.
2. **a)** A description of a made up character's face.
   b) A description of a made up character's clothes.
   c) A description of whether a made up character is tall or short.
   d) A description of a made up character's voice.
   e) A description of a made up character's behaviour.
   f) A description of a made up character's special powers.
3. 2 marks: the main problem of the story identified and its resolution described. Both present for 2 marks; one correct for 1 mark.

Pages 84–85
Challenge 1
1. My dad is very tall and my mum is small <u>but he has short hair and a beard</u>. They like <u>the beach</u>. I went out there with them and saw it, <u>but it was hot</u>. We picked up sea glass. The underlined pieces make sense on their own, but not as part of one sentence. The fact that dad has short hair and a beard does not depend on how tall he or mum is! The fact that it was hot doesn't depend on going to the beach either so that would have been better as a separate sentence.
2. **a)** I **can't** do my **work** because it is **too** hard.
   b) We went to the **beach** and had **some** ice **cream**.
   c) My favourite cake is **chocolate** cake but my sister likes **ginger** cake best.

Challenge 2
1. 3 marks: a paragraph consisting of at least three sentences about the child's favourite animal which make sense. All present for 3 marks; two correct for 2 marks, one correct for 1 mark.

2. **a)** I like **cats** best because they are furry.
   b) My baby brothers **Oliver** and **James** are noisy.

Challenge 3
1. 3 marks: a paragraph consisting of at least three sentences about the child's school which make sense. All present for 3 marks; two correct for 2 marks, one correct for 1 mark.
2. **To wrap** a present you need paper**,** tape**, scissors** and a **label**. Put the present on the paper and cut it **to** the **right** size. Tape it shut and fold over the edges**.** Make sure everything looks **neat**.

Pages 86–87
Progress Test 3
1. Any sensible answer; some suggestions have been given.
   a) sp + ace
   b) sp + it
   c) sp + ade
   d) sp + ider
2. Any instructions on how to make pizza. For example, Ingredients: base, cheese, tomato sauce, vegetables
   Method: • Spread the tomato sauce over the base
   • Cover with grated cheese.
   • Sprinkle chopped vegetables over it.
3. **a)** Elle saw <u>a swing, a slide and a see-saw</u>.
   b) Jake saw <u>a bird, a dog, a mouse and a butterfly</u>.
   c) David saw <u>a man, a woman, a girl, a boy and a baby</u>.
4. 2 marks: a review of the child's favourite café or restaurant, including responses to at least two of the questions. Both present for 2 marks; one correct for 1 mark.
5. **a)** At **knight** / ⟨night⟩, I sleep in my bed.
   b) Will you **bee** / ⟨be⟩ ready soon?
   c) Please come over **hear** / ⟨here⟩
   d) We ⟨ate⟩ / **eight** our dinner all up.
6. **a)** Any appropriate simile for 'cat' – such as 'like a tiny tiger'.
   b) Any appropriate simile for 'water' – such as 'like a blue silk sheet'.
   c) Any appropriate simile for 'wind' – such as 'like a roaring monster'.
   d) Any appropriate simile for 'lizard' – such as 'like a perfect baby dragon'.
7. **a)** Any appropriate metaphor for 'rain' – such as 'falling grey beads'.

b) Any appropriate metaphor for 'sea' – such as 'The sea was a sheet of glass'.

c) Any appropriate metaphor for 'mouse' – such as 'The mouse was a tiny grey bear'.

d) Any appropriate metaphor for 'sugar' – such as 'The sugar was crystals of glitter, shining in the sun'.

8. I wanted **to** go **to** the woods **for** a walk but it was **raining**. I decided **to** go anyway and put on my **wellies** and my raincoat. It wasn't **too** wet in the end so that was good **really**.

Pages 90–91
Challenge 1
1. a) **T**he sun is so bright we need our sunglasses.
   b) **W**e went to play football in the park.
   c) **M**y sister likes apple juice but I prefer pineapple juice.
2. **S**he saw the dog steal my sausage. **I**t sneaked up to the table and grabbed it. **I**t was really naughty. **N**ow there are no sausages left. **T**he dog will have to stay in the garden at teatime.
Challenge 2
1. a) **T**he raindrops fell into the puddle with a loud plop.
   b) **T**he garden is full of bugs like spiders and worms.
   c) **W**e built a model using old junk.
2. a) Ⓘsaw a starfish in the rockpool.
   b) Ⓐmouse ran across the garden and hid in the wall.
   c) Ⓜy friend likes playing games about space, so we do that a lot.
Challenge 3
1. a) Any correct answer.
   b) Any correct answer.
2. I love making pizza for my friends. I bake the base first and then add tomato sauce. I add sliced vegetables next. Last of all I add cheese and herbs before my dad helps me to bake it in the oven.

Pages 92–93
Challenge 1
1. a) I can't wait to see you!
   b) It's nearly my birthday and I could pop with excitement!
   c) That is too hot!
2. **D**o you like cats? **P**erhaps you prefer dogs? **D**o you like rabbits best? **D**o you think it is easier to have a pet that you do not need to walk every day? **D**o you know what each pet eats?

Do you know what sort of bed they need? **I**t is important for your pet to be comfortable.
Challenge 2
1. I went into my bedroom to look for my skates. I looked under the bed and saw a spider scuttling towards me! I don't know who was more surprised – me or the spider! I screamed and my mum ran in to see what was wrong. **S**he laughed when I told her and we caught the spider and put it outside in the garden where it would be safe.
2. a) **W**ould you like a lolly?
   b) **S**he is going to be okay.
   c) **W**ho wants to go to the beach?
Challenge 3
1. a)–c) Any suitable sentences where one ends in a full stop, another ends in a quotation mark and another that ends in an exclamation mark.

Pages 94–95
Challenge 1
1. a) Sara bought oranges, apples, bananas, strawberries **and** grapes at the market.
   b) Julie had marbles, string, a pencil **and** a bar of chocolate in her pocket.
   c) At the circus I saw clowns, a trapeze artist, acrobats **and** jugglers.
   d) Collies, pugs, spaniels **and** huskies are all breeds of dog.
Challenge 2
1. a) I have dolls, trains, teddies **and** puzzles in my toy box.
   b) We need to feed the dogs, cats, rabbits **and** guinea pigs.
   c) In my paint box there are red, green, yellow, white, blue **and** black paints.
   d) Don't forget to bring your lunch, notebook, pens **and** coat on the trip.
Challenge 3
1. a) Cake, bread, scones and buns.
   b) Red, pink, purple, white and brown.
   c) Monkeys, elephants, bears, tigers and lions.

Pages 96–97
Challenge 1
1. a) walk
   b) shout
   c) jump
2. a) fly
   b) smile
   c) laugh

Answers

Challenge 2
1. a) skipping or eating
   b) eating
   c) barks or ate
2.

I love		shining
The sun is		swimming
It is		snowing

Challenge 3
1. a) The snow is <u>sparkling</u>.
   b) I am <u>dropping</u> a plate.
   c) I am <u>sliding</u> down the hill.
2. a) The wind is <u>blowing</u>.
   b) My cat is <u>purring</u> so loud right now that I can't sleep!
   c) The mouse is <u>running</u> quickly so the cat cannot catch her.

Pages 98–99
Challenge 1
1. a) The wind <u>blew</u> hard yesterday!
   b) Yesterday, there <u>were</u> three rabbits in the garden.
   c) Yesterday, Suki <u>was</u> drinking orange juice.
2.

smile		ran
look		looked
run		smiled

Challenge 2
1. a)–c) Any sensible answers.
2. a) cr**ied**
   b) shriek**ed**
   c) walk**ed**

Challenge 3
1. a) laugh**ed**
   b) sew**ed**
   c) plant**ed**
2. a) swam
   b) ran
   c) sang

Pages 100–101
Challenge 1
1. a) The horses' saddles are grey.
   b) The girls' bags are heavy.
   c) The cats' toys were fluffy.
   d) The singers' dressing rooms were cold.
   e) The teachers' cars were all covered in snow.
   f) The boys' coats are black.

2. a) couldn't
   b) didn't
   c) isn't

Challenge 2
1. a) children's
   b) women's
   c) men's
2. a) won't
   b) can't
   c) I'd

Challenge 3
1. a) doctors'
   b) houses'
   c) farmers'
   d) women's
   e) men's
   f) children's
2. a) can't
   b) I'd /She'd / He'd / They'd
   c) She's / He's
   d) didn't
   e) they've
   f) Don't

Pages 102–103
Challenge 1
1. a) My dog has bad breath **and he** needs his nails trimmed.
   b) My favourite cake is chocolate flavour **and my** favourite drink is orange squash.
2. a) Kassy can go to the park **when he**r class is over.
   b) I will go to the beach **when it** is a sunny day.

Challenge 2
1. a) Should I stay at home **or s**hould I go out?
   b) I could wear a dress **or** I could wear a skirt.
2. a) Tom has a stomach ache **because** he ate too much ice cream.
   b) I opened the window **because** it was hot.

Challenge 3
1. a)–c) Three appropriate sentences that use 'but' to join ideas.
2. a)–c) Three appropriate sentences that use 'if' to join ideas.

Pages 104–105
Challenge 1
1. a) dogs, monkeys
   b) mouse, onion, badger
   c) girl, table, ladybird

2. a) <u>The cat</u> meowed.
   b) <u>The woman</u> smiled.
3. a) rough
   b) fluffy

Challenge 2
1. a) Brighton ✓ England ✓
   b) Italy ✓ Raj ✓
   c) Marie ✓
2. a)–c) Appropriate noun phrases.
3. a)–c) Appropriate adjectives.

Challenge 3
1. a) P
   b) C
   c) P
2. a)–c) Appropriate expanded noun phrases using nouns from the box.
3. a)–c) Appropriate adjectives.

Pages 106–107
Challenge 1
1. a) run, laugh
   b) sit, jump
   c) sleep, leap
2. a) loudly
   b) early
   c) here

Challenge 2
1. a) My cat **chased** the bird.
   b) A man **carried** the bag up the stairs.
   c) The flag **fluttered** in the breeze.
   d) The man **waved** the fly away from his face.
   e) A mouse **ate** the cheese.
   f) The fire **burned** brightly.
2. a) The fireworks flashed **brightly** in the sky.
   b) The snake slithered **silently** across the grass.
   c) The water lapped **softly** across the sand.

Challenge 3
1. a)–c) Appropriate verbs.
2. a)–b) Appropriate sentences with the verbs underlined.
3. a)–c) Appropriate adverbs inserted.
4. a)–b) Appropriate sentences each containing an adverb that has been underlined.

Pages 108–111
Progress Test 4
1. 2 marks: relevant and appropriate instructions, the three elements of the picture. Both present for 2 marks; one correct for 1 mark.

2. a) The baby's eyes were green.
   b) The girl's hat was purple.
   c) The dog's tail wagged as she ate her bone.
3. a) It went bang! It was really loud! I love fireworks! They made the baby cry though! They were so pretty! I jumped when the last one went off! It was so loud!
   b) That really hurt! I wish you hadn't stepped on me! You should look where you are going! It hurt so much!
   c) Don't do that! It's really mean! I wish you would think about things before you do them! It was so silly!

Any of these exclamation marks would be 'correct' but point out to your child that it is not good to use too many exclamation marks in their writing, or they lose their power to emphasise things.

4. a) pink
   b) glittery
   c) tiny
   d) massive
   e) ancient
5. a) The <u>smooth</u> pebble rolled down the hill.
   b) The <u>juicy</u> pineapple squirted my face!
   c) The <u>tiny</u> mouse scuttled under the chair.
   d) My <u>old</u> jumper fell apart.
6. 4 marks: four memories explained clearly. All present for 4 marks; three correct for 3 marks, two correct for 2 marks, one correct for 1 mark.
7. a) The hedgehog snuffled <u>noisily</u>.
   b) The crab ran <u>quickly</u> across the sand.
   c) The gem glittered <u>brightly</u> in the sunshine.
   d) The slug slithered <u>slowly</u> up the wall.
   e) The mermaid sat <u>lazily</u> on a rock, watching the shore.
8. a) teachers'
   b) farmers'
   c) women's
   d) men's
   e) children's
9. a) won't
   b) shan't
   c) can't
   d) isn't
   e) I'm

Progress Test Charts

Progress Test 1

Q	Topic	✓ or ✗	See Page
1	Listening and Asking Questions		12
2	Describing and Explaining		14
3	Describing and Explaining		14
4	Describing and Explaining		14
5	Contractions and Apostrophes		26
6	Telling Stories and Narrating		16
7	Reading Non-fiction		36
8	Getting Information from Instructions and Lists		44

Progress Test 2

Q	Topic	✓ or ✗	See Page
1	Breaking Words into Segments		52
2	Discussing Favourite Words and Phrases		30
3	Homophones		56
4	Contractions and Apostrophes		26
5	Spelling – The Ends of Words		60
6	Spelling – The Ends of Words		60
7	Handwriting – Joins		66
8	Syllables		54

Progress Test 3

Q	Topic	✓ or ✗	See Page
1	Breaking Words into Segments		52
2	Writing for Different Purposes – Instructions, Lists and Letters		72
3	Writing for Different Purposes – Instructions, Lists and Letters		72
4	Describing and Explaining, Writing About Real Events		14, 74
5	Homophones		56
6	Similes and Metaphors		80
7	Similes and Metaphors		80
8	Does it Makes Sense?		84

Progress Test 4

Q	Topic	✓ or ✗	See Page
1	Writing for Different Purposes – Instructions, Lists and Letters		72
2	Contractions and Apostrophes		26, 100
3	Question Marks and Exclamation Marks		92
4	Nouns, Noun Phrases and Adjectives		104
5	Nouns, Noun Phrases and Adjectives		104
6	Describing and Explaining, Writing About Real Events		14, 74
7	Verbs and Adverbs		106
8	Contractions and Apostrophes		26, 100
9	Contractions and Apostrophes		26, 100

What am I doing well in? _____

_____

What do I need to improve? _____

_____

Notes